CW00953179

Affiliate Marketing Secrets

How to Start a Profitable Affiliate Marketing Business and Generate Passive Income Online, Even as a Complete Beginner

PUBLISHED BY: Chandler Wright

Table of Contents

Your Free Gift 4

Chapter 1- What is Affiliate Marketing? 5

Chapter 2- Benefits of Affiliate Marketing 11

Chapter 3- Common Types of Affiliate Marketing Channels 26

Chapter 4- How to get Started with Affiliate Marketing 41

Chapter 5- Examples of Affiliate Marketing 80

Chapter 6- How to Achieve $10,000 a month through
Affiliate Marketing 95

Chapter 7- Tips to Becoming a Successful Affiliate Marketer
.... 104

Chapter 8- Top Affiliate Marketing Trends of 2019 114

Chapter 9 - Tools to Help you in Affiliate Marketing 125

Conclusion 134

Thank You 135

Your Free Gift

As a way of saying thanks for your purchase, I wanted to offer you two free bonuses - *"The Fastest Way to Make Money with Affiliate Marketing"* and *"Top 10 Affiliate Offers to Promote"* cheat sheets, exclusive to the readers of this book.

To get instant access just go to:

https://theartofmastery.com/chandler-free-gift

Inside the cheat sheets, you will discover:

- The fastest way to start generating income with affiliate marketing
- My top 10 favorite affiliate offers to promote for high recurring commissions
- Access to a FREE live training where you will learn:
- how one affiliate marketer built a $500,000 a month business all while traveling the world...
- The 3-step system to eliminate risk and instability in your online business
- The 7 biggest mistakes affiliates make in making money online
- How tech companies are giving away <u>FREE MONEY</u> to help you start
- And much more...

Chapter 1- What is Affiliate Marketing?

Make money while you sleep. That is the ultimate dream, right?

If you are considering a passive income stream, one great way to do this goal is through Affiliate Marketing. The idea behind affiliate marketing is that you promote someone else's products or services using an affiliate network. In turn, you earn a commission, if any products are purchased based on your marketing.

The mechanism behind affiliate marketing is revenue sharing. For example, if you have a product or service that you want to sell more and target to a bigger audience, you can offer financial incentives to promoters using an affiliate program. If you have no product and just want to make money, then you can be the promoter of the product that you feel has substantial value and can earn income as an affiliate marketer.

In this book, we will endeavor to uncover the basic secrets of affiliate marketing, the simple strategies, and how you can get started on it. But first, let's look at the definition of affiliate marketing. To put it plainly, affiliate marketing is cycle of getting commissions or a cut for promoting a product or service that is not owned or produced by you. This person can be a company, organization, or a sole entrepreneur. You find a product that you know and like, promote it to your channels and audience, and accrue profit for every sale made.

What components are involved in affiliate marketing?

Essentially, there are 3 components to affiliate marketing. They include:

1- The Affiliate

2- The advertiser

3- The Affiliate network

Who is the Affiliate?

The affiliate is the individual who does the promoting or the website's owner. Anyone can build a website nowadays is suitable for the business; however, when building a website for marketing purposes, consideration should also go into marketing the specific website. In this website, you will find details or reviews about a product or service that is sold on the advertiser's website. The affiliate's website cross links to the product page of the advertiser using a link known as affiliate link. This special link specifically indicates the link's source to the advertiser.

What is the advertiser?

The advertiser refers to the business that sells the product or service. It could be an individual, a company, an organization, as long as there's an online commerce site.

What is the affiliate network?

The affiliate network refers to the tracking cookie that is dropped into the buyer's browser when he or she visits an advertiser's website. This cookie is dropped when a buyer clicks on any affiliate links on the affiliate's website. This cookie is the reason that makes affiliate marketing possible because they send the payment to the affiliate.

Still unsure what affiliate marketing looks like? Let's see it in action.

Let's assume that Jane is an affiliate. She has a website that showcases products about woodworking. She even has a blog that she shares videos of her latest woodwork as well as images of her crafts and the places she visits to purchase her materials. She also provides in-depth information on the best and worst places to get resources for woodworking.

Her information provided also gives reviews with links to the advertiser's website where the recommended woodworking supplies can be purchased. The key is that the link included denotes no ordinary link.

An ordinary link would be like: janewoodworks.com/best-wood-supply-store

In actual fact, an affiliate link would like: janewoodworks.com/best-wood-supply-store/affiliateID112783

If a visitor goes to Jane's site and decides to purchase a product after reading her reviews about places to buy the best supplies, then Jane as the affiliate will be rewarded with a commission for referring a buyer to the advertiser's site.

No matter when a buyer decides to purchase a product from the advertiser's site, maybe in a week after reading the review or in two weeks, the affiliate will still be rewarded the commission simply because of the cookie used on the affiliate network that remains on the browser.

How long do these cookies stay?

A question affiliate marketers always have involves how long do these cookies stay and when will they disappear? There are ways that this would happen:

1-If the buyer decides to clear his or her cookie cache on their browsers, then this step can be done either manually or using tools such as CCleaner.

2- The cookie also can expire. Most cookies on affiliate networks have a 30-day period. However, vast majority of advertisers now opt for lifetime cookies. So even if someone opts to purchase a product one month after reading the review, the affiliate will still get paid.

The Affiliate's Advantage

The advantages are quite obvious for the affiliate marketing business model. To have the opportunity to 'sell stock' effectively, without the hassle of any of the costs or responsibilities of buying, storing or manufacturing items is a plus point that is quite liberating. Plus, when working with high-paying networks, the profits can be substantial.

Affiliate marketing, when done correctly, can turn into an extremely profitable passive income. It is most likely that you will need and also want to keep your eye on the price: and if you can get into the business to bring in substantial income, you may be able to outsource plenty of seemingly routine tasks to freelancers in the long run.

Plenty of affiliate marketers stumble at the point where they believe that success in affiliate marketing is easy and quick. Affiliate marketing takes work and hours of learning, as well as the willingness and commitment to adapt to the changing situations of things. Besides the obvious advantage of running your own business, affiliate marketing also offers the individual, you, the freedom to work online anywhere, anytime and also have the freedom to choose how hard you want to work. As affiliate marketers, you also have the probability of acquiring some freebies from advertisers who want to boost brand awareness.

A website is critical to the affiliate marketer. Depending on the topic, the marketer has the ability to give a company enough exposure to the point where he or she will ask you to trial one's products for free.

The Advertiser's Advantage

So what's in it for advertisers? The very same business model for affiliate marketing can yield huge potential for the sales of their products and services. Paying only when you see or receive the results desire is an excellent way to advertise and requires very minimal budget to begin. This is an ideal model for start-up business when they have little funding to market their brands.

Apart from this benefit, what could be better than having thousands of websites promoting your product? This is an example of online 'word-of-mouth' marketing at work.

People are talking about your products online through reviews and blog posts, so what better way to get your brand out there?

How much can you earn from affiliate marketing?

Your income will depend entirely on a few massive factors such as:

1- The reliability and efficiency of the affiliate network you are working with currently.

2- The advertisers' conversion rates and commission levels.3- The level of commitment within your investment

4- The depth of willingness and knowledge to learn all you need to know about your niche to succeed

These commissions and networks vary widely. There will be new affiliates that can take over a year just to make their first sale, but with the right training, acquiring knowledge as well as persistence, you can earn a lot of money.

Through affiliate marketing, you can easily make some pretty impressive earnings. Top earners earns multiple millions of dollars a year.

This all sounds great but don't be quick to hand in your resignation letter just yet. Before you can go on full speed on affiliate marketing, laying the foundations of affiliate marketing is imperative. It will definitely take some time, but once you get the gears running, it will be easier for you to better judge whether you want to leave your day job or not.

Chapter 2- Benefits of Affiliate Marketing

When you become an affiliate marketer, you automatically become an independent proprietor of a chosen product or service from the generic to the niche, on behalf of the vendors. When you become an affiliate marketer, this also means you now have absolute freedom to create online presence. You get to call the shots on when or where your job needs to get done, how to optimize your marketing process, as well as how to reach your customers.

As discovered from chapter 1, affiliate marketing is an online business model that is great to start off if you want passive income online. It is a low-cost but high-profit industry. Affiliate marketing gives you the flexibility to earn how every much you want. It all depends on the determination you have, the approach you take as well, as the affiliate strategy applied.

Before we explore the strategies, it is worth to explore the pros and cons list so you are aware of what you're heading into, what works and what doesn't. So let's dive into it.

Advantages of Affiliate Marketing

- ### It's a billion-dollar business

There's no denying that affiliate marketing is a billion-dollar business. Plus, with the Internet, it seems that it will continue to prosper. Because it is a big industry, there's plenty of potential and it also means there's unexplored territory- products and services that have not yet been created or advertised.

- **It involves extremely low costs**

A relatively easy to join business model, affiliate marketing offers no barriers. This is one of its biggest attractions. The biggest hurdle to take is to decide to do it or not and when you say YES, the next steps are relatively easy. Your main asset is your affiliate marketing website or even becoming an affiliate marketer without a website. Next involves about choosing a familiar niche. Finally, the last step encompasses i finding the right products or services that appeal to your market. By signing up to an affiliate program, you're ready to begin!

- **You don't need excellent business prowess**

The big mantra here is practice makes perfect in affiliate marketing. You do not need to be a marketing whiz to be able to become an affiliate. This is the other great thing about affiliate marketing- you can learn along the way. Affiliate marketing is about testing both organic and paid advertising to see what works and what doesn't for your product niche. What's more, you also have plenty of options to run and manage the affiliate program. You will need to test several sequences to see which performs well or which combination of strategies perform effectively with your target market. From here on, once you've found a good formula, it's all about optimizing and repeating successful patterns to obtain the best results.

- **It has low investment costs**

When you start out, the operating expenses of affiliate marketing is next to nothing, especially when you compare it to other industries. Most of your work is online, which means you do not need office space. Your home is good enough to operate from and then you will only need basic utilities such as a good and stable internet connection, electricity and ISP subscriptions. You may also need to spend on other expenses such as web hosting capacities as well as some minor costs related to website design. This can be done once you have a better grasp of your affiliate business. Other costs related to your affiliate business only takes place later on in the growth cycle such as renting out a co-working space when you have freelancers working for you or if you have a partner. These costs can be controlled- it is up to you if you want it or not.

- **Second source of income**

You do not need to leave your current job to make it in affiliate marketing, even if you can afford it. The choice is yours. You can make affiliate marketing as a side business and accrue extra income.

- **Convenience and Flexibility**

To increase your income, you can create and conduct multiple affiliate campaigns on different affiliate websites to market your links. This way, you can abandon the ones that are performing poorly and pay more attention to the channels that are performing well. You can utilize many different affiliate programs. Selecting various products from the chosen niche is the preferred route for many affiliate marketers and it also enables them to test these niches. You can promote each one on a daily basis.

You will also know which product sells better and which one doesn't. If one is difficult to sell, the other might be easier and more profitable. If a single program is not working out for you, you are also not obligated to stay in it. In sum, this approach will help to mitigate the risks of failure and maximize the opportunity for a marketer to earn a good income. Do not put all your eggs in one basket- keeping your portfolio diverse is the best route.

- **Customer Service is not your priority**

As an affiliate, you do not need to deal with customer service. No managing customers or worrying about retaining customers for you. All you need to care about is your commission so when you do get a post-sale query, you can just pass this request to the merchant's site. Of course if you do want to deal with customer service, then you can make a mutually beneficial rate with your merchant. User-generated content for your reviews can definitely boost your SEO so you if you want do customer service, then you need to have a comprehensive system of replying to these queries as fast and as accurate as possible. Customer service is at the end of the day- YOUR CALL! No one will impose this on you or expect it from you.

- **The independence**

You have the flexibility of making your working environment the way you want it to be and according to your own wishes. You can be working anywhere, from a cafe in Hungary to an island in Thailand. All you need is internet connection. You decide where your office should be. As an affiliate marketer, there are no company regulations to follow or daily meetings to attend or weekly reports to hand in. You set the rules yourself; you decide what time you start, what time you finish, and what your dress code is.

- **Marketing kits are your disposal**

Any marketing materials are provided by vendors, so you do not need to fork out any money to produce your banners or any other promotional materials.

- **Reaping profits even while you are asleep**

Another strong feature of becoming an affiliate marketer is the idea of gaining passive income while you sleep. It is possible for you to get money while you sleep because people are still buying products after clicking on your affiliate links. But to get there, remember there is some work involved.

- **The Sky's the limit**

There are very different ways to market your affiliate programs. You can set up a website, you can set up a blog, you can create affiliate emails, you can create PPC campaigns. The options are endless. You can also use the power of social media and platforms such as Facebook and Quora to market your affiliate products. You can also do a combination of organic and paid advertising to cross-promote your campaigns.

- **Sole proprietorship**

As an affiliate marketer, you are basically a freelancer and you still need to establish your business activity. The advantage is the costs, since mobile phones or laptops can be claimed as tax write-offs.

- **It's a flexible working schedule**

Being your own boss means setting your own rules and framework as well as daily working schedule. If anything unexpected comes up, you can always change your timetable to meet or fit in unexpected activities or events. You can also decide to take a vacation anytime you want.

- **Performance based income**

Some marketers think of this as a disadvantage. The thing is, affiliate marketing will determine if you are good at online marketing. To be able to get a good stream of income, you need to be able to be good at writing reviews, writing articles, recording videos as well as marketing your site. It's hard work still but all of these just bring you more revenue which is why affiliate marketing is a performance based income. The more you do, the more money you'll get.

Persistence is the essential factor here. It takes time to amass traffic to your site before you can make money from, it but once you've struck gold, it's a yellow brick road all the way to success!

The Disadvantages of Affiliate Marketing

- **You Don't Control Affiliate Marketing Programs**

You are dependent on the program that you choose, the merchant's rules as well as the conditions set. You will not be able to adjust the terms on your own. All you can to is communicate the need for any adjustments that you see from your perspective such as giving discounts and being more visible on social media. The merchant then takes the necessary steps to implement changes.

- **You Cannot Control Your Competition**

Depending on your particular industry, the competition differs. There are strong benefits of joining an affiliate program such as the high-profit-low-cost investments and no immediate expertise required. But those that are highly talented from the same niche can give you a fierce competition and are an obvious danger to your own performance and survival. This however should not scare you. No matter what kind of business you go into, there will always be someone doing better than you are, so the key here is to be persistence and work smart!

- **You do not have control over your customer base**

Once a referral has been made, a repeating customer is highly unlikely to purchase from you again. This customer may just do it directly from the affiliate vendor to repeat their purchase again. That is the truth about affiliate businesses. While you commit to driving new leads again and again, recurring customers are unlikely to visit your site. This is why most marketers do not bother with after-sales services and leave it to the vendor itself to provide.

You can however engage with marketing affiliate programs that do provide commissions for return customers.

- **No Guarantee of Revenue**

Unfortunately, this is a major setback. The pay-per-performance can be both an amazing opportunity as well as a significant risk. No one can promise that working in the affiliate marketer will be easy and do not be fooled if you think that you will be able to earn your expected revenue immediately. It is a challenge that you have to face, and you need to put all your efforts into increasing this opportunity. It is difficult to estimate how much money you will make on affiliate marketing.

- **Freelance Jobs are not for Everyone**

Yes, freelance jobs are not for everyone. Some people prefer to have a safe and stable 9 to 5 job, but for many people, freelance opportunities present a different set of freedom. On one side, you have flexibility, no meetings, you can work anywhere and be your own boss. But this also means that you will face some form of loneliness as well as stagnation. You might feel like you do not have motivation to work. There are ways that you can prevent this though. You can start working in a co-shared space with or working in a space outside your home.

With plenty of offices now going on cloud, there are co-working spaces available, coffee shops designed for the freelancer in mind as well as buildings that enable you do rent a desk or a space just for quick meetings and for freelancers just like yourself. You can just look around to see what suits you best.

- **Quantity Approach**

Some marketers end up doing the spammy marketing approaches and while this has some kind of benefit, it is a short-sighted campaign because it only produces misleading content everywhere. Marketers may get small wins, but they are very short-lived.

Once you end up in the black hat of affiliate marketing methods and false advertising, it will crush your growth. You will lose credibility and you will also put your merchant at risk. Doing spam affiliate campaigns will also lead you to a breakup from the vendor's side and then, you will break your commission.

Quality is always better than quantity so focus on long-term, quality solutions in creating your affiliate strategy. Invest in quality leads as this gives better investment for the time and effort you put in. Plus, it will also bring you sustainable and recurring revenue. Be legit because it is the only way you can gain trust with your vendors as well as other affiliates in the business.

- **It's Possible to Hijack Affiliate Links**

Hijacking affiliate links is a method used to deprive affiliates of the commission which is that they should rightfully be earning. Hijacking is done by bypassing the full link where a person types the affiliate link in a browser instead of clicking on the links. The other way is by removing the affiliate ID in the link and adding their own. While hijacking is still pretty rare, there are a few bad apples who will resort to this method to get commission. When it happens, you cannot get your commission back unfortunately. You can report it and ensure your website has the necessary security.

Now that we know the advantages and disadvantages of affiliate marketing, it gives us a deeper understanding of the nature of this business. It will help you, the affiliate, in making objective business decisions and it will also help you build a capable business model to decide if this is the right kind of business for you. If you look at this list, there are more benefits than disadvantages which is a great thing. There will also be risks and issues with a business, but it is up to us to be aware of these things and learn from them in order to avoid making mistakes. Speaking of mistakes, let's look at the common mistakes that beginner affiliate marketers make, which you can avoid.

Rookie Mistakes in Affiliate Marketing

- **Picking the Wrong product**

There are plenty of products out there for you to choose. But choosing the right one to market and plan your affiliate marketing campaign around will ultimately be the deciding factor in your success or failure. Selecting a product wisely is an absolute must. When you hone the right product and the right niche, you will automatically be geared to create marketing activities around it. Whatever campaigns you create, they will be authentic because you know the product and you know what it takes to sell it.

A rookie mistake made when it comes to picking a product is that the affiliate picks a prominent product just because they think there is money behind it or because it is easy to sell. The product you choose must drive you on its own otherwise no matter how popular it is, you will not be able to market it because you are not invested in it. Your affiliate business will not excite you in the long run. You do not want to make yourself a slave to your money that comes from a product you have little interest in and one that you are only doing out of 'getting money.. Pick something you are passionate about and one that you know. It will prove to be worthwhile in the long run as it will be something you can sustain.

- **You are promoting too many products**

It is not wrong to promote various different products. After all, you need diversity. When you choose the products you want for your own affiliate collection, many rookies make the mistake of selecting too many of them. Being overly ambitious and over-enthusiastic is not the approach you want to go for when you start. Over time, you will be less enthusiastic to promote and market your products because you will likely be too distracted by trying to achieve too many things at one time.

Selling too many products at one go will eat up valuable time and decrease your value in the long run. When this happens, it ultimately leads to fewer affiliate sales. What you can do though is to pick selected products and to focus all your motivation and enthusiasm on them. You would be able to commit more time with a few, selected products and then turn your endorsements and reviews into the right actions-which are making sales. Over time when you have a better handle of the affiliate business, you can add more products to your portfolio and grow your business. Just ensure that you continually give each campaign the individual attention it deserves to succeed.

- **Designing and operating a poor website**

There is no excuse anymore to have a bad-quality website, especially when there are plenty of services that allow you to create beautiful websites simply by dragging and dropping elements. Making websites is easier nowadays than ever.

So what happens when you have a poor quality website? Low quality sites mean low sales volume- it's a quick reaction. While you do not need to create a high-end, high-tech website with plenty of amazing user friendly interfaces, you still need to provide a basic, accessible and friendly site that will turn visits and clicks into immediate sales. Plenty of platforms enable you to create free sites, but then again, taking the option of investing in a website with a good domain name and hosting capabilities can take your sales from zero to hero.

You will want to avoid a slow or unresponsive website. Remember that it takes only 3 seconds to make a first impression online so make it worth it. Messy templates and an unorganized site will also get your customers frustrated and lose interest in what you have to sell. They also will not be coming back because they have associated your site with all things negative.

You will want to provide a nice online shopping environment, easy navigation and an overall pleasant experience when customers browse your site-much like how you would be providing a nice space to shop if it was a regular shopping store.

When you build your site, keep these things in mind. We all like shopping on a website that provides easy access. So when designing a website, answer these questions:

- Is it easy to navigate?

- Is your website easy to find?

- Does your website enable you to quickly and easily find the section?

- Does it highlight the products?

- Are there clear calls to action?

- Is your website simple enough to find information?

- Is your website responsive?

Your site does not need to have flashy graphics to attract users. It just needs to be intuitive and simply enough to be interactive and easy to navigate. Identify what you want on your site, what products you want to display and the content you want to have on your site. Make sure that your website also personifies the kind of products you are selling.

- **Not having high-quality regular content**
High-quality and updated content is an essential part of affiliate marketing. Heck, it is an integral part of any kind of marketing. Users nowadays are very used to high-quality images and content, so having low resolution photos and poor descriptions only damper your ability to sell.
This rookie mistake is a major problem that is very often overlooked. Content is important in marketing and no matter what your site is made out for, whether it is comparisons, product reviews, blog articles- all of these contributes to your online sales either directly or indirectly. Do not make the error of posting content that has no actionable item or is not insightful. When writing a piece of content, always make sure that there is a solution or a purpose. Put yourself in the shoes of your potential buyers and imagine what kind of content they seek. You want people to get hooked on stories and cool facts, not random ramblings.

Good content alone is not enough. You must also ensure that you churn out content on a regular frequency. When your users are interested in what you have to say, they will be expecting some form of consistency in terms of your uploads-they want to know more and you have the job of getting them consistently engaged.

- **Not tracking the performance of your website**

As someone new to the business of affiliate marketing, knowing how your website is doing with the users are coming is helpful so you know what they click on, where they click on, how long are they on your site and what buttons attract them. Part of marketing is optimizing your data and tracking it. You will want to see the cause and effects that happen when you do tracking so you know what works for you. You can use various tracking tools such as Google Analytics, Hubspot or Sprout Social. The website you choose to host your content should also be able to give you plenty of analytics for you to see.

- **Not continuously learning**

As an affiliate marketer, you must always keep abreast of the things and trends that are happening in your line of business. Changes take place rapidly in the online world and you need to keep up with the standards. It is a challenge to always stay updated but reading and subscribing to business news and marketing blogs will help stay informed. Educate yourself and read online guides to ensure that you know what is happening. Trends take place frequently and some work for your business while some don't but knowing them helps you navigate through the business of affiliate marketing as smoothly as possible.

- **Not being brave to try new things**

It is imperative to test out the various tools and versions of copy and content, media and campaigns when you want to sell your products. The online world has plenty of online marketing capacities that are easy and fast to set up. Delivering the same kinds of messages just because they worked before does not mean that you will have continued success. While some users may take the bait, most will eventually get bored and this will lead to slumped sales. You must keep things fresh in terms of content as well as campaigns to reach out to new target markets.

Never accept the status quo. Explore a variety of marketing opportunities and experiment towards perfection and when you do this, do not forget to conduct A/B testing. You can test out plain emails versus HTML emails, you can also test out different subject lines to see which one hooks your client base. You can also try different approaches towards the same pain points for the same buyer persona.

Testing out is fun because it helps you to evaluate your campaigns effectively. Now you know the advantages and disadvantages as well as the rookie mistakes made in affiliate marketing.

Are you hungry for more? Let's examine the next chapter.

Chapter 3- Common Types of Affiliate Marketing Channels

So what are the types of affiliate marketing you can try? With affiliate marketing, it is important that you understand the fundamentals of what makes up affiliate marketing and the difference between programs and networks. Affiliate programs are individual merchants, whereas networks are a grouping of merchants under one umbrella.

Affiliate marketing, on the other hand, is basically a relationship between the affiliate, the merchant and the consumer. As we know, the affiliate is YOU- the person who promotes a product or service from the merchant in exchange for a commission. The merchant is the person you partner with - the one with a business and pays you to help them promote his or her business.

The affiliate works with the merchant on a contractual basis and provides the merchant with creative data that they can incorporate into their website in order to promote their product or service. The consumer bit is pretty straightforward. It is any individual who takes an action after seeing an advertisement. This action is clicking on affiliate links to make a purchase. This act is known as a conversion. In any affiliate channel you decide to take, having an online base- whether a website or a blog, is a good way to start. In this chapter, we will look at the different types of affiliate marketing channels available so you can make a better decision of which one works for you and is right for your needs and expertise.

Essentially, there are three types of channels:

1. **Unattached affiliate marketing**
2. **Related affiliate marketing**
3. **Involved affiliate marketing**

Unattached Affiliate Marketing

Unattached affiliate marketing is your basic pay-per-click affiliate marketing campaign. Here, you do not have any authority or need not even show presence on the product niche that you promote. You need not worry about having any connection whatsoever between the product and the consumer.

All you have to do is place an affiliate link using Google Adwords or Facebook Ads and this way, you hope that someone will click on your link, go to the merchant's site and purchase a product, thus earning you a commission. This type of affiliate marketing is extremely attractive, as it requires little to no presence. Plus, it's less of a hassle, compared to opening a blog or a website. This type of marketing is not really a business model but it is a straightforward income generating model. This model eliminates the pressure of meeting people and instead focuses more on the potential income, rather than the customers.

Related affiliate marketing

With related affiliate marketing, you have some level of presence online, meaning through a blog or a podcast, on social media or even on YouTube. You create affiliate links to the products related to your niche. Placing affiliate links on your site that are related to your niche is a more comprehensive and decent strategy to earn a little bit more income from your blog or website.

You can place this either in the sidebar or in a banner format or even text link them into your blog posts. Because you have a blog or a website, the credibility is higher, and you also get to decide where to place these ads.

If you use this type of marketing, then it is best to work on a product or service that you know and like. This is because people coming to your site, whether your blog or website, are under the impression that you know your product and you know what you are writing about and that you are in a way, an industry expert.

People will trust you and decide to purchase the products that you have linked on your site. Do not promote anything that you have not tried or loved on your own. Support a product because you really like it and you'll have a better chance of increasing your online presence because people will sense and read your honesty.

If you do not promote the right products, even if you know the owner of the product or service or you think that this product may be a great fit, you run the risk of losing the trust you have built among the online community of readers and users who flock to your website in search for credible information.

It takes a lot of work to build authority and trust, so a one bad affiliate link can potentially ruin this trust. So when you recommend a product, make sure you trust this product and the merchant selling this product.

Involved Affiliate Marketing

In this type of marketing, you really need to use a product or service and truly believe in it and you personally recommend it to your audience. This is not done in a banner format or through Google Adwords or a section on your website with the title 'Recommended Resources'. This is deeper than that. You are involved as you should be when talking about a product or service and this type of affiliate marketing produces the more sustainable of results. Your involvement and experience with the product or service is the reason why people flock to your site and why your site is at the top of Google search ranking results.

In this type of marketing, the level of responsibility is high. You also have plenty of authority and influence over your followers, which is why you need to ensure that your content is both helpful as well as honest. This marketing is the complete opposite of unattached affiliate marketing, where the affiliate is not even seen by the consumer for a transaction to take place. In unattached affiliate marketing, you use money to make money.

With involved affiliate marketing, your readers or consumers have their eyes and ears on you. You use your reputation, authority and trust to get recommendations, use it and get paid in the form of commissions. So which do you think works well for you? Either approach you take involves some form of advantage and disadvantage as well as varying degrees of responsibility and credibility. No matter which approach you take, you will see some form of success through your affiliate marketing.

Affiliate Marketing Channels based on the degree of involvement:

- **Webmasters - Related affiliate marketing**

Webmasters are individuals who own their own sites and also those who build websites. They are thousands and thousands of webmasters and they all have different levels of expertise. Most of these webmasters are signed into sharesale or CJ. These are affiliate programs that affiliates can partner.

- **Search Affiliates- Related affiliate marketing**

Search Affiliates are individuals that spend their own money to leverage search engines, Facebook advertising and other Paid advertising models to generate ROI for other affiliate offers and also for themselves. These kinds of affiliates have a strong entrepreneurial spirit and are business-minded. They love testing many different capacities of affiliate marketing. You can engage with search affiliates as long as there are rules in place and they use recommended procedures to generate the right kind of traffic as well as revenue.

- **Bloggers - Related affiliate marketing**

Blogging is another kind of affiliate marketing that is great for those who can write and want to continuously post information about a company and also reviews about new products. It is one of the most popular options for affiliate channels. For bloggers, all they need to do is get samples of products from merchants, try them out, and write a review (preferably a positive one), which will help spread information about these products. Credibility is a key issue with blogging and the more people read about your reviews or content about a merchant, the higher this content will rank on the search engine. Blogging can help increase traffic for the merchant and provide genuine number of conversions for the merchant.

- **Coupon Sites- Unattached affiliate marketing**

 Coupons are always in demand no matter what the economic condition. What's not to like with saving a few extra bucks, right? Coupon sites make for really crucial and popular affiliate sites for a merchant's business. If you are planning on venturing as an affiliate here, keep in mind that coupon sites are like a double-edged sword. They have their advantages as well as disadvantages. The advantage here is that you can use these sites to direct traffic to your own website and thus channel these to the merchant's site but enabling affiliate links on the coupons.

The downside of using coupon sites is that they capitalize on organic rankings that are connected to your company's name and the coupon code. Coupon sites usually have a member base that is established, and it can be quite beneficial to you as an affiliate who wants to increase traffic to one's sites.

- **Review Sites- Involved affiliate marketing**

Review sites are another popular option for affiliate marketers. For this option, you need a website that can review different products in a specific niche. Affiliates that use this kind of channel usually deal with flower companies, dating companies, internet marketing companies and phone companies, taking up at least five to eight different advertisers and putting them on a site then running an organic search or paid search throughout all the pages that feature various reviews. The affiliate will earn commissions when a business is referred to any of these advertisers, making the review site large and converting demography of the marketing affiliates.

- **Loyalty Portals- Involved affiliate marketing**

In loyalty portals, companies usually have a very large membership base and they are able to expose your offer as an advertiser to members and these offers sometimes contain a cash-back policy. There are plenty of loyalty portals in the market and most conduct themselves on a performance-basis. A merchant can select any of these loyalty portals to improve his or her business.

- **Incentive Programs- Involved affiliate marketing**

Incentive programs have their good things as well as the bad things about them. The great thing about incentive programs is that as an affiliate, you can get loads of traffic from prospective buyers but the disadvantage here is that other affiliates can take action on your ads and can skew down the quality of leads and sales. There is also the problem with virtual currency through the use of social networking. Users can earn virtual currency using their social channels and then you also get some companies that leverage their affiliate advertisers to allow these users to redeem their virtual cash to make purchases. During the process, they also attain a good savings deal.

Most Popular Affiliate Networks of 2019

Speaking about affiliate networks, there are plenty out there online, and choosing the right one will make your road to success slightly easier. In this section, we will look at the most used or most popular affiliate networks to check out. This list is not complete because there are numerous out there, but it's good to know which networks are available for you to choose.

ShareaSale

ShareASale is among the most popular of affiliate networks and it has been in business for over 15 years. Their technology makes them an exclusive affiliate marketing network and they often receive accolades for efficiency, speed as well as accuracy. Plus, they are known as an honest and fair business within the affiliate marketing business.

PeerFly

This award-winning and international online affiliate platform removes the risks, headaches and costs usually associated with traditional forms of online advertising by channeling that burden across thousands of professional affiliates who get paid only when a measurable transaction takes place, such as a sale or a lead.

Rakuten

Formerly known as Buy.com, Rakuten has rebranded and has now transformed into an affiliate marketing giant. It ranks among the top three e-commerce sites in the world featuring over 90,000 products from 38,500 online shop owners. Rakuten also boasts over 18 million customers. It is known for its flagship B2B2C model and the e-commerce site Rakuten Ichiba has the title of largest e-commerce site in Japan. It also has the world's largest volume of sales.

ReviMedia

This online lead generation network focuses on operated campaigns for home services, insurance and financial verticals as well as exclusive advertiser's campaigns that is primarily focused in the US. They also have their very own proprietary lead management platform that is called Px.com, which gives users quality scoring for each lead and insight into performance by enabling key demographic info. ReviMedia is also flexible in running campaigns in various integrations. ReviMedia also has extreme transparency with their clients, something they are proud of as well as flexible payment terms. It also gives their advertising partners access to their huge direct publisher network of over 2,000 publishers.

RevenueWire

A global e-commerce platform, RevenueWire is specifically catered to companies that sell digital products and all of them online. It uses industry-leading services like Affiliate Wire, and their e-commerce platform is used in more than 120 countries.

Payolee_Partners

This is an affiliate program that is specifically designed for online marketers that join and promote Payolee. Payolee is an online payment service that is best for small business. Relatively new to the affiliate market, Payolee empowers small businesses to accept one-time or even recurring payment options on their website. As an affiliate of Payolee, you can earn 55% of monthly commissions for every customer that you refer.

Clickbank

Clickbank is another huge affiliate network that has been in the game for over 17 years. It is one of the largest online retailers with a library of over 6 million unique products that reach a total of 200 million customers worldwide.

Wide Markets

This affiliate network provides unique cross-channel advertising capabilities for e-commerce businesses. This network owns Wide Markets Fashion, Wide Markets Media as well as Wide Markets eStores and Wide Markets eTickets. Using this network, advertisers can use it to sell their services, their goods and their products through native products created by Wide Markets. Publishers on the other hand benefit from a native method to monetize their online assets to find higher conversion rates. This network supports the Performance Marketing Association and is an active Champion Member.

CJ Affiliate by Conversant

CJ Affiliate was known as the Commission Junction before, but they have now reached an average of 1 million monthly customers using their site to go shopping online through their vast affiliate marketing network. CJ Affiliate also networks with companies such as the Commission Junction, Greystripe, Dotomi, ValueClick Media as well as Mediaplex.

Amazon Associates

Amazon.com, a huge name in the affiliate marketing business needs no introduction. It is an American e-commerce and cloud computing company that is headquartered in Washington. Being the largest Internet-based retailer in the US, Amazon.com's affiliate network enables you to tap into millions of products to advertise to your customers.

CPAmatica

CPAmatica, with its rather interesting name, is based in Kyiv, Ukraine. It is an affiliate network that operates throughout North and South America, Asia as well as Europe. It began as a one-person company in 2015 with its founder, Evgeniy Prima who was interested in helping others expand their business with a smarter approach. This network specializes in an innovative and simple approach, one that is deemed as more humanized.

AffiBank

AffiBank is a private affiliate network that you can use to promote a wide range of products from cryptocurrency to health products. It gives 75% commissions on each sale made using PayPal. Payment is made twice a month. AffiBank adds products on a consistent basis and it also has the 'AffiBank School' where affiliates can learn and access tutorials to learn affiliate marketing. It also helps affiliates to succeed in their promotional efforts. Joining this network is free and it also includes a $10 bonus into your account.

Leadbit

Leadbit manages thousands of digital and affiliate marketing projects. This network consists of 400 professionals in Moscow as well as others from around the world. Their ideology is monetizing at every possible niche. They are also very open to working with their publishers and also providing them with exclusive offers.

Affiliate Partners Ltd.

This is an affiliate network in the financial industry and it is known for giving among the highest payouts (CPA) up to $600 for niches such as gaming, casino, trading as well as sales funnels. Affiliate Partners makes affiliate marketing easier simply because they have a professional team that is reachable 24/7 through email and Skype.

CrakRevenue

CrakRevenue is also another long-time player in the industry. The CPA network has proved to be one of the most trustworthy platforms for affiliates throughout the world. They have 700+ quality offers that marketers to choose from and even from exclusives from MyFreeCams. CrakRevenue is a definite answer for affiliates who want to enjoy some of the industry's cutting-edge tools such as Surveys and Smartlinks as well as for those interested in joining a caring network.

eBay

Another well-known brand for e-commerce but not known as an affiliate network. eBay has now been online for over 20 years and its Partner Network also provides exceptional class tools, reporting as well as tracking.

Avangate

Another player in the digital commerce field, Avangate is backed by a cloud platform and it focuses on subscription billing and online commerce as well as global payments for Saas, Online Services and Software companies. More than 4000 digital business in over 180 countries use Avangate such as Kaspersky Lab, Spyrix, Brocade and Bitdefender as well as Absolute Software.

Flexoffers

This is a premiere affiliate network that builds profitable partnerships that are mutually beneficial between skilled, strategic as well as trustworthy online publishers. They also have a robust relationship with over 5,000 popular advertising spanning all verticals. Flexoffers have 10 over years of experience in the affiliate marketing industry and they also over excellent customer service, data delivery tools and dependable payments. Their game is flexibility when it comes to affiliate success FlexOffers is also ranked at the top 8 overall in CPS Networks 2015 Blue Book Survey.

Avantlink

Avantlink is known for its industry-leading platform for affiliate referrals. It works extremely hard to maintain its cutting edge upgrades and updates as well as introducing rapid implementation of new tools and technology. Their emphasis is on quality, rather than merely quantity.

Commission Factory

Commission Factory strives to provide performance-based marketing available to everyone without the steep learning curve. They do this to get more people involved and be successful in affiliate marketing. This platform is designed to specifically target a sense of collaboration between Affiliates, Agencies as well as Merchants to grow a substantial and beneficial partnership. Commission Factory has a fast growing user base that enables companies of various sizes to be part of the performance-based marketing.

AdCombo

Another CPA Marketing Network, AdCombo uses its own in-house technology system that enables marketers to customize their advertising campaigns to reach a targeted audience all over the world. AdCombo aims and hits their targets to encourage strategic and lucrative partnerships between publishers as well as advertisers.

Olavivo

As a boutique affiliate network, Olavivo focuses on e-commerce, beauty, health and cryptocurrency verticals. Their network promises transparency, dedication, as well as unique technological capabilities using the highest professional service.

Chapter 4- How to get Started with Affiliate Marketing

In this chapter, we will review the most basic and required steps to get started. You will go through 5 steps which embody:

- **Step 1- Finding your Niche in Affiliate Marketing**

- **Step 2: Create a Website or A Blog**
  Step 3: Choosing and Signing up for an Affiliate Program

- **Step 4: Creating Content and Using Social Media for Promotions**

- **Step 5- Optimizing your Content**

Keep in mind that these steps are the most basic in order to excel in affiliate marketing. Without these essentials, there is no way you can even call yourself an affiliate marketer. Essentials are important to start anything.

Step 1- Finding your Niche in Affiliate Marketing

It may sound overwhelming to find your niche in business because there are plenty of areas where you can specialize. While it does sound overwhelming, it is not hard as there are a few methods that you can employ to find that perfect niche that would give you profits. Here are some methods t for determining the right niche:

Tip #1- Brainstorming

Brainstorming is always effective for practically anything you need to work on- ideas, solutions, methods and finding the right niche. To begin brainstorming ideas for your niches, meet up with your business partner or like-minded friends who will be able to help you or someone you trust. Friends and family who know you and your business partner are the most ideal. Next, you will want to block off time to focus on your brainstorming- so set a meeting, time and date for this goal. When you meet, one of the things to think about is the items that you or your business partner or friends have bought online or recently purchased. Write these things down, even if they perplex you. There will be tons of niches that are profitable but that does not mean you should rush into picking one for your affiliate marketing business. When you have your niches, list them and filter them according to:

- Competition: Look out for other affiliate marketing business and explore the kinds of products that are oversaturated. You do not want to get into selling these.

- Loyalty: Avoid getting into niches that are dominated by national brand

- Pricing: The higher the price of the product, the higher to get the margin profits

- Weight: The winning combo is a high-priced product, but it has low shipping weights.

- Returns: Do not go for products that have different sizes and style preferences- they usually come with high return rates

Tip #2- Research, compare and evaluate trends

eBay is one of the recommended places to check whether items sell online but do not use eBay to determine the price of your products as eBay's prices are relatively low.

Once you get onto eBay, you will want to research and identify the products in the different niches in the higher-priced bracket, the ones that are expensive so it can be anything like $50 or $200 or $500 depending on the product. When you obtain your search results, allow them to show 'completed listings'. Completed lists shows items in red or green, red denotes the item did not sell and green reflects sold.

Look at the items only for the products you are considering to niche in- it is okay to go over this list a few times until you identify about 20 products within your niche that sell out almost always- at least 10 units a day. From here, request for price lists from various suppliers, get shipping quotes from customs brokers as well as storage capacities for a product.

Tip #3- Utilize Amazon

Being the world's largest retailer, Amazon sells everything imaginable. Because of this dominance, Amazon is one of the best things on the Internet to find profitable niches and other amazing possibilities that you never thought of. You can find profitable niches using Amazon and it is one way to attain this objective.

Firstly, just click on the 'All' tab which is located on the left side of the primary search toolbar. Upon clicking on it, you will see niches or a list of categories

- Click on a category that interests you and clicks on 'Go'.

- When the new page pops up, you will see on the left, a list of 'sub-niches'

- By clicking on a subcategory, you will then see more specific sub-niches

- You now have specific niches! You can go down this list if you really desire.

Amazon is also a great place to help you in a specific niche as well as the product that sells the best. You can also choose 'best sellers' from the navigation bar located just right under the search bar at the top of the page. You can see all the items that are currently selling the best.

Tip #4- Put on your Marketer Cap

One of the best things you can sell with drop shipping is to sell EXPENSIVE items.

The average affiliate marketing profit is about 20% of your total sales. You make 20% profit on an item that is $1,000 which is $200 or 20% on an item that is $10 which makes you $2. If you want to start making money, start selling the big toys. Sounds simple, but in truth, you will need to do more research. You will also need to identify potential future competition, which involve other online retailers who are selling the items you want to sell.

The roadblock here is there is no way to determine how much money a retailer makes on each and every sale at this point unless you use a MAP procedure.

Should I choose passion or money in a niche?

It really depends on you. To some people, starting a business in affiliate marketing also means that they can work on a product or be doing business that they love. Whereas to others, they find motivation the more money they see in their bank account and they don't care what they sell.

The truth is, you want to make a profit for any kind of venture or business you are in. So you will most likely look into a balancing act of pursuing your passion and creating a successful profit line.

Having said that, you still need to have some kind of interest in the product that you are selling because it will keep you motivated to explore even further on your audience needs, which will also help you to better align your content. When it comes to pursuing your passion, it doesn't necessarily mean that you'd be successful.

So how do we balance the two?

Passion does lead the way. Finding profitable niches to things, items and products that you are passionate about not only makes your bank account healthy but also it makes you have fun and love what you do. To help you discover your passion, if you already have not, let's take a look at niches that are based on your passions. Here are some questions you can ask yourself:

- What kind of blogs and websites do you interact with and visit the most?

- What kind of pages or accounts do you follow on social media that you enjoy?

- Which online stores do you usually purchase from?

- What do you think are your biggest obsessions?

- What kind of products do you usually collect or buy most frequently?

Create a shortlist of products based on the answers you give to the questions above. Next, if you want to choose a niche based on how much money you can make, then you might want to ask yourself this set of questions:

- Which niches hold the biggest audiences?

- Which online retailers have been increasing in popularity lately? And what products do they sell? (Answer these questions focusing on a few specific niche-based retailers instead of big names like Amazon)

- Which products are the most popular right now?

- Which products have huge profit margins?

Evergreen Niches vs Trending Niches

An evergreen niche is a niche that most retailers would like-it stands the test of time. Things like gaming, beauty, fashion, and weight loss are extremely evergreen niches. However, on the other hand, trending niches have instant profits and surge, but they also fall in popularity pretty fast.

Tools that you can use for finding a Niche Market

There are a variety of different tools that you can use to create shortlists of niche ideas in order to determine if you can see any niches that show signs of being highly profitable or aligned within your passions.

First, start your search with these:

- Oberlo
- Amazon
- AliExpress
- Treadhunter

On all these websites, you can easily find the trending niches. Keep your eye out for niches that keep coming up and also try to find potential sub-niches that you deem as interesting that might complement each other.

Trending Products Blog Posts

Another tip is to assess for updated product lists. Oberlo is one such company that regularly shares updated product lists to ensure that they are always at the forefront of today's most popular products. These lists can also help you determine your specific niche. Besides, keep an eye out for blog posts with lists such as:

- 20 of the best gardening tools to have in 2018
- 30 Fail-proof Business ideas to make money in 2018
- Best Buy Beauty Products for Summer 2018
- Top 10 Polishes To Get your Car Shining like Brand new

Check out the products mentioned, as well as the affiliate marketing products being sold and the business ideas related to them:

Wikipedia's List of Hobbies

Wikipedia's list of hobbies is a great way to find a niche of practically anything that you can think of from hobbies to passion, from crocheting to baton twirling, resin art to golfing, furniture restoration and terrariums- you will be surprised to find an extremely extensive list of both indoor and outdoor hobbies. Assess the lists to determine if there are any hobbies that compliment your passions or research to find profitable niches within these categories. Some are hobbies are popular enough to have a large market of followers, so you can actually build an entire store dedicated to selling these products or the items that help these hobbyists work on their passions.

The amazing thing about hobbies is that you will have like-minded people join groups and spend the money to pursue their hobbies. This itself gains you an audience you can immediately sell to. Some of the hobbies on the list that you can build e-commerce stores for include:

- Jewelry making
- Astrology
- Do it yourself
- Fashion
- Flower arranging
- Gardening
- Magic
- Pet
- Various fitness niches
- Baking

Google Trends

Yes, Google Trends is another tool you can use to discover your niche. What you want to look out for are niches that have a stable growth, no matter how slight. Here is a list you can check out- Google Trends.

Do you need to be an expert in finding your niche?

You do not necessarily need to be a niche, but some experience will help you a long way. It may be slightly harder to build a successful brand without having some kind of niche experience, although it is not entirely impossible.

Alternatively, you can also fake it till you make it. This means that you can just find the right target audience through Facebook ads as well. You can also engage influencers using the power of Instagram to build an audience as this can lead to sales. Having some idea about the niche you are getting into will also help you create content that resonates with your audience. No experience may render it harder to reach them and bring that traffic to your store.

On the other hand, you can also outsource these blog writing tasks to ghostwriters or someone equivalent. But most entrepreneurs do this, especially when starting out to keep costs low. As mentioned previously, getting into selling a product you somewhat like and having some expertise in the niche can help motivate you, in the long run, to sustain your business, especially if the money isn't hitting the profit margins like you desire.

FB Search

Another tool you can use is FB search and this tool can help you determine the amount of engagement your posts actually get. You can also use this as a competitor analysis tool so you can see the posts of both your competitors, as well as customers, make. You can also look up at the brands that are within your nice. Search using specific keywords to search. Your search will turn up based on people, pages, photos, videos, links, and marketplace. When you look at these pages, you can see the number of followers. It will also help you understand the kind of frequency your Facebook posts need to be, which is somewhere between 1-2 posts per day to maintain a competitive advantage and scale quickly.

Browsing the pages that come up in your search also gives you an idea of the direction of your marketing strategy, looking through photos helps you understand the kind of material you need to create and the markets you can target.

Continue your research

Here are several other things to consider before you start building your store. You want to make sure that you have an audience for your niche even before you were spending hours on marketing your website and buying ads online. Here's a quick list of what to look for:

- What kind of social platforms do people market your niche?

- Are there dedicated Facebook groups for your niche?

- Are there targeting options you can use on Facebook for this niche?

- What kind of forums exist for people to discuss the niche?

- Do people host events for this niche?

- Do influencers post about this niche?

- Are there fans for your niche?

Pinterest, YouTube, Instagram and of course Facebook are all popular places to look if your niches are talked about on these platforms. It is always better to put your content where it is seen, heard and speaks because there is where your audience spends time on.

Another thing is, all these platforms have one element in common. They are all heavy on visuals which means, stunning images and video attract your audience faster.

Step 2: Create a Website or A Blog

Designing a website or a blog requires planning, and it needs a robust and good plan. Although setting a website or blog through Wordpress is free, you'd still want something that is lasting and memorable, even if this website or blog is for personal use.

On a piece of paper, just use at least 20 minutes to articulate your Mission Statement. You will want to have a few things determined for your site, so you have the focus to your site and you know the content you want on it.

Here are a few things to establish:

- What will you do with your site?
- What kind of content do you want on it?
- Who do you want to read this?
- How often do you plan on posting and adding content?

Depending on what your site is supposed to do, you will need to consider what kind of information you are willing to share and post. You would also want to include some contact information, so your visitors can contact you-unless you don't want them to do so.

Choosing the Right Domain Name

The domain name and the domain extension go hand in hand. Once you have decided on your domain extension, you need to figure out what you'd like to call your site which will be your domain. Your domain name is what your website's URL will consist of when someone types it into the browser's address bar.

Here are a few crucial points to consider when devising with your Domain Name:

- Matching Names: Essentially the name of your site as well as the URL must match.

- Short: So it's easier to remember and can be typed into the browser

- Consistent Branding: Your domain is a reflection of your brand. Keep it consistent and memorable.

- Memorable: Well, a website must be easy to remember and memorable, so you want it to stick the first time when your visitors come to your site.

- Catchy: It must be easy to pronounce and roll off the tongue easily. Your domain name must also describe what you do.

- Includes Keywords: You want it to be Search Engine Optimized (SEO).

Essentially, you want it to be easy to remember and easy to type. Your domain name must correspond with what your business does or what your personal online agenda is for your site.

Customizing and Personalizing

To make your site 100% your own, you can choose to personalize and customize the theme. Usually, customization is done on the fonts, the colors, and other simple design elements, without altering the layout of the site.

To customize the theme you have selected, you can go back to the Appearance section and choose the Customize link. Here, you have the option of doing a variety of things to your site to make it sync in with your branding needs. Usually, most themes allow you to change the logo, the colors and backgrounds, the fonts, the header image, the menus and the widgets.

In this chapter, we will investigate the various ways in which you can customize your site based on what can be changed. If you are not experienced in coding, it is best to leave the customization to the selected options. But if you do know coding and can take your site's customization to another level, then go ahead- there is no stopping you and the sky's the limit!

Step 3: Choosing and Signing up for an Affiliate Program

When you sign up for an affiliate program, you will need to ensure that it fits your needs, your site as well as your audience. There are affiliate programs for whatever route you go for and for whatever products you choose, whether you're a blogger for electronic products, a review site for vacation home rentals, or even coupon codes for makeup.

Stick with programs that suit your needs and your site

When you find an affiliate program, it does not mean you need to sign up for it immediately. When you become an affiliate marketer, your credibility becomes extremely crucial and it also depends on how involved you are in the program you choose. The involvement you have in the program can become even greater when you start pushing the boundaries based the content you engage your users with. Marketing products and services that stay true to their selling features will bring you trusted, loyal fans; and doing the opposite will make you less of a star.

When you choose an affiliate program, stick with ones that are a natural fit for you and for your site. You will find that it is much easier to keep growing your audience with this approach, and you will also yield a higher rate in sales.

Assess the Customer Service Experience

When choosing an affiliate program, do a little bit of research on its customer service, You want to know what it is like for customers to deal with product or service issues, which will give you a good idea on how much value the merchant site places on customer service and how much value they place on customers. Merchants that value their customers will offer good customer service, which is a good sign for you as an affiliate. Everyone wants to make money online but to ensure that the income you get is consistent and sustainable, do things ethically, even if it means it will take a longer time to achieve the target you want. You want to promote a product or service that is ethical as well, so if you will not recommend a product or service to your own family, then it is best not to sign up for a program that you will not recommend to your site visitors.

Place yourself in your users' shoes- you should also be hesitant to purchase from a merchant that has bad reviews and recommendations right? So keep thing in mind when sourcing for a program to sign up for. Signing up for a program that has questionable reviews and low quality products would ultimately affect your own bottom line. Why does this happen? Because unhappy customers will return products and they will never want to buy from the same site again. They will also post their review somewhere on the Internet. Your merchant's credibility also affects you, so choose wisely.

The Commission Rate

Commission rates matter: and while this facet should not be the only thing to consider when signing up, it is part and parcel of making your decision of choosing an affiliate program. Commission rates are generally small but the more sales you make, the more they add up. If you have found a program that offers a smaller pay percentage consistently on particular items compared to others, then you are just wasting your time. You need to research commission rates for various products on different affiliate programs before you sign up with them. Different programs offer different rates- look for one that has the best rate with the best payment term and the best terms and conditions.

Average Order Size

The average order size may be a piece of information that is hard to find, but it will be useful for you to determine, even if they do not offer this information. The average order size gives you an idea of how business works on their site and what kind of opportunities you will have to gain more money. These little extras will add up to your bottom line. For instance, sites that offer free shipping for purchases over a certain amount means that buyers will be encouraged to buy a little extra to get their money's worth on the shipping bonus. And if you promote these items on your site, you get a little extra incentive to gain more money because the chances of buying are higher.

Payment Threshold

You must also get to know the kind of payment threshold involved with your program especially when you have different affiliate programs and networks that you are interested in. It makes the decision-making easier. Affiliate programs are individual merchants, whereas networks denote groups of merchants under an umbrella.

The payment threshold for the program and the network could be identical, but you are more likely to meet the threshold in a network at a much faster rate as it will include your commissions from multiple merchants. The profits you earn add up much faster than acquiring sales from just one merchant. This means you get paid more often from different merchants.

However, it does not mean you should avoid individual programs. It also depends on the product you have chosen as well as your audience. Choosing to stick to a program may be beneficial for those who do not have that much of time promoting several different programs from various different merchants. Also, a program may suit an affiliate who wants to make an average side income of a few hundred a month.

Understanding the threshold for programs or networks is essential nonetheless as it will give you a better understanding of how much you can potentially make and how else can you maximize your earnings. Not reaching your threshold also means you may be penalized for it.

Cookie Length

When doing your research on affiliate programs, analyze the cookie length. For some affiliates, the cookie or tracking code lasts for a few hours while for some, it could be months. If a customer makes a sales sale while they cookie is still there, you will earn a commission even if it wasn't a direct sale from your site. A longer cookie length however does not mean it is a better affiliate program. It is just useful knowledge to know what your program entails and how you can utilize it to gain more profits. Your cookie length must relate with your product- some products take smaller decision making time to purchase whereas some take longer. Your cookie length needs to match the consumer's purchasing habit.

Terms and Conditions of the Affiliate Program

You will want the terms and conditions of your chosen program articulated in a clear fashion. You don't want unnecessary surprises and hurdles just to get paid. You must read and understand your choice of program before signing up so you know what you are agreeing to from payment terms, cookie length, and payment threshold, and so on. Weed out the bad programs by reading the fine print, so you can make the best decision with the best programs available.

Step 4: Creating Content and Using Social Media To Promote Your Website

There is no such way a business can survive without social media. Practically every type of business, big or small with the intention of moving forward, is adapting and seeking new opportunities and customers need to have at least one social media account.

From our previous chapter, we know that Facebook takes the cake when it comes to social media dominance so much, so that even an old business serving a small neighborhood community has at least a Facebook mention or a street address on Facebook.

Social media is a great tool in generating leads, and as a marketer, you should pay a good amount of attention in amplifying your social media presence so that it can play a significant role in generating leads in your marketing campaigns and strategies. Social media can drive niche web traffic from those that are actively seeking the kind of information you are projecting. Using social media monitoring, advertising, networking and content creation will bring you the kind of leads your need to maximize your online sales.

A) Using Social Media to Build Strong Networking Ties

Harnessing the power of social media takes time. To generate leads, you must invest in interaction, affection, communication and time. How do you create ties?

1- Follow prospects on Twitter and LinkedIn

Following prospects and industry leaders in this platform help builds authority, and it also produces interaction. Users visiting your Twitter or LinkedIn pages will see the kind of people you follow and create a perception that you are keen and passionate in the line of business you are in. You as the account holder would be able to communicate, share, engage, like and comment on these prospects pages. All these things will be viewed by current and potential customers.

2- Make friends on Facebook

You'd be surprised how people view friend requests on Facebook. It is sort of like giving a business card to people- you offer it to them with the hopes of either receiving a call or so that they will remember you when a business opportunity arises.

3- Utilize Google Hangout with Industry Leaders

Google Hangout is the professional version of Facebook. When you do share email contact with other business leads of a company whether an employee, the CEO, marketing executive, and directors - Hangout with them on Google.

Share ideas, presentations, conduct virtual training classes, and invite them for company cocktail events and the like. It presents a more interpersonal approach from one employee to another.

4- Host a webinar

Hosting a webinar creates authority, increases trust and positive perception on your brand. Hosting webinars also lure the niche crowd you are targeting which increases the chances of this select crowd signing up for your service or purchasing your product.

5- Answer questions on your social accounts

Opening social media accounts and not interacting with your community and clients is social media suicide. Social media gives consumers a means of communicating with brands on a more personal level. Not answering any questions or comments posted on your account or not even participating in discussions on your page does not create a wholesome image for your brand.

B) Influence connections for content sharing

Publishing and sharing content exemplifies one of the best ways to increase lead generation. Here are some great ideas to help you to create content:

6- Writing ebooks and include forms

Ebooks, whether free or paid, provide an excellent way to share your content with your target audience. Usually, a short accompanying blog list post would help in increasing the download of the ebook, too. The blog post itself entices the reader, enables sharing, and fosters keywords optimization. Writing ebooks also increase your authority on the subject and credibility.

7- Retweet

Found a tweet that promotes your product or service? Retweet it. Locate a negative comment on your product or service? Read no.5.

8- Make visual content

In our previous chapter, we discovered that Pinterest was the biggest network featuring shared content. Optimize your content to make it easily shared on Pinterest. Visual content also makes the amount of time to make a decision to share or comment or tag someone lesser, thus increasing conversion rates.

9- Don't always talk about you, your product or your service

Nobody wants to constantly read about things that you sell or do. Sometimes, it helps to create content on helpful information. For example, if you sell cars, write content about how to maintain different car engines or where is the best place to get car parts. Link with other service providers into your post, and you'll work on no.2 on this list.

10- Optimize for mobile viewing

As a result of smartphones, information is now in the palm of our hands. Any content you create has to be optimized for mobile viewing first and desktop second. Your consumers are more likely to view your newsletters, product updates, emails, statutes, and tweets via mobile then they will be on their desktop. One of the things to consider when optimizing for mobile viewing is also when to publish your content, so the chances are higher for your clientele to pick up their phones and read it. 3 am is not the time, in case you are wondering.

11- Utilize Slideshare

Increase your credibility and authority on your subject matter and industry by creating relevant and shareable content on Slideshare. Again, this content must not be about your product or service because then it's just selling your stuff. Talk about information that would subtly help your business. For example, if you sell cars, then mention things like DIY servicing, how to care for second-hand vehicles, how to change black oil and so on. People will naturally flock to your site at the end of the presentation for more details.

C) Utilize social media monitoring

Listening to your audience on social media helps to uncover

plenty of information on how receptive they are towards your brand and how your brand relates to them. Listening in this sense involves seeing the interaction between consumer and brand and reacting to this through offering information or expertise helps increase the sales, without the pressure of selling. Here's how to monitor for lead opportunities:

12- Monitor industry trends

It is essential to keep up with trends in your industry to stay at the top of your game. Trends can help make your product or service more visible. For example, if you sell shoes and the latest trends are fringe products, then highlight shoes in this category through your newsletters and blog posts or, link an article featuring fringed items and connect it with your product.

13- Monitor discussions about your product category

Reddit, Buzzfeed, CNET and Google Alerts are great places to monitor conversations of your product category. Google Alerts, for example, gives you alerts on any news items that are related to your keyword search. Staying updated on what's happening in your industry helps you not only to make more informed marketing decisions, but it also allows you to interact proactively with your customer base.

14- Monitor questions and conversations about your product category

Questions and conversations about your product category

regularly help you tweak your product to better suit your target market's needs. Conversations often takes place at comment sections in social network such as Instagram, YouTube, Facebook and even commerce sites such as Amazon and EBay. Just keep an eye out on what your audience is saying.

D)   Use social ads to generate leads

Of course paid advertising and sponsored Tweets as well as promoted content on Instagram, Facebook and Twitter can help generate leads. It will assist if you have a new product or service or an event that you would like to reach out to new audiences.

 Here are ten examples of how to do it:

> 15- Use a Facebook ads & Promoted tweets to drive traffic to your website.

Facebook ads and promoted tweets are perfect for new businesses entering this incredibly popular social network platform. If you have a new product or a new event you want to promote, use the ads. Facebook and Twitter ads are relatively cheap, and you can also create ads to target specific type of audiences based on their location, age and even, content that they search on the Internet.

> 16- Create an ad on LinkedIn

LinkedIn ads are perfect for promoting webinars, seminars, training as well as talks. Use ads on LinkedIn wisely for the right type of content because the people you are targeting are different from those on social media accounts like Snapchat and Facebook. If professionals or business people are what you are looking for, then LinkedIn is the place to advertise business content that you know will help them.

17- Make ads for Pinterest

Within the US, Pinterest's audience is made up of 52% Millennials, 68% of women aged 25 to 54 and 69% of moms and 36% of dads. Knowing this piece of information, tweak your ads to be visually appealing and made for this target audience. Clothes, shoes, baby products, vintage accessories, and art are the best kind of products to be advertised on Pinterest. No matter what you do, make sure your headline corresponds with your images.

18- Advertise on forums

Depending on what industry your product or service is in, advertise in them. There is a forum for practically everything on the internet from Crockpots to homemade baby foods, GoPro cameras, hand woven silk, drones, short story writing, second-hand furniture, garage sale, old books and novels and so much more. Understanding your clientele also means knowing where they 'hang-out' online and where they get their information. People often tend to rely on information found on forums because it's mostly from other users who have utilized them before.

E)   Search Engine Optimization (SEO)

Last but not least is SEO, which is a huge driver to your online sites. A combination of the right keywords, social media content, blog content and a good website can all boost your SEO. With better SEO, you are able to reach out to your target audience much easier as they can find you more easily.

Always remember to ensure that this is always on your checklist when it comes to Search Engine Optimization:

- Cross-linking your post to your Facebook or Twitter accounts (or both)

- Using appropriate keywords on your LinkedIn page

- Applying relevant keywords in your headlines

- Utilizing tagging and specific keywords for your images

- Sharing your ebooks with relevant keywords and phrases

- Integrating visual content by using infographics, YouTube videos, and Instagram-worthy images

- Connect and share through Google +

Bottom Line

Like it or hate it, social media is here to stay. As the year goes by, there will be newer platforms that will make their ways into consumers' smartphones, and mobile applications; in turn, businesses must keep evolving with this technology. Social media has presented a relatively cheap, fast and convenient way to share, post, update, and advertise to the masses and brands must take advantage of this. One of the major takeaways for social media is that it allows a deeper and more personalized connection between brands and consumers, which also mean brands must be ready to react, respond, and connect with their target audience at any given time.

By connecting with your audience, you enable them to see a more human side of your brand, and that also means you get to let your brand personality shine.

Millennial want this. Millennials want a genuine connection with the things they use, the brands they come into contact with and the products and services they use.

This is why cheesy stock photos do not relate anymore to the consumers of today.

If managing several social media accounts give you a headache, move on to the next chapter to discover what tools that you can utilize to maximize your productivity, marketing and also managing several accounts at one go.

Step 5- Optimizing your Content

Increase Traffic with Better Headlines

Online marketing and content go hand in hand. As you know by now, content is a key decision maker on whether a user will click on a call to action or a blog post, an article, a video or an image. What is it that makes certain content more clickable and shareable than another?

This chapter focuses on data mined by <u>CoSchedule</u> on over 1 million headlines of blogs and social media content. The research was conducted on headlines that have at least a total of 100 shares across major social networks. Below are the results of their findings. As a result, you can learn how to tweak or change the headlines in your own content.

Result 1: Majority of content does not get shared that much

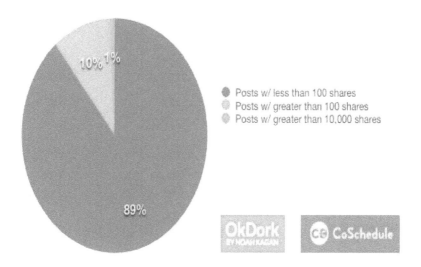

The results here are astounding. 89% of the content you create is never shared for more than 100 times. This is a major indication for content creators and online marketers working together that things need to be done differently.

But what about the 10% that was shared 100 times and the 1% that was shared more than 10,000 times? What is it that made those headlines top performing? Knowing these essentials will help you to create your own content and position your website among the top high-performing sites on the Internet in your selected field.

Result 2: What common words/phrases are used in highly-shared headlines?

Most Popular Words/Phrases In Highly-Shared Headlines

Word/Phrase	# of uses	% of headlines
List Post	787	11.10%
You/Your	478	6.74%
Free/Giveaway	255	3.60%
How To	205	2.89%
DIY	197	2.78%
I/Me/My	153	2.16%
Easy	137	1.93%
Win	104	1.47%
New	97	1.37%
Ways	75	1.06%
Why	60	0.85%
Video	51	0.72%
The Most	17	0.24%

CoSchedule also compiled a list of common words and phrases used often in headlines to figure out what made them more attractive to share. As you can see, the results again are telling.

Takeaway #1 – List Posts are in Demand

It goes to show that people find list posts are shared much faster 1,000 times. This despite the fact that list posts only make up a total of 5% of the posts actually written by marketers. It reveals that content creators don't create enough of these types of posts in the first place.

Takeaway #2 – Identify with You and Your

Headlines that utilized the words 'you' were shared extremely well and very frequently. Posts that used 'I' or "Me" were shared three times less. It shows that content written in the second person point of view resonates with the reader as if the content is speaking directly to the reader. It makes it ideal to be shared compared to content that comes from a first person view, and that usually means it isn't about the reader but about someone else. It also denotes that readers like to envision themselves in what they are reading.

Takeaway #3 – Help Your Readers Imagine A Better Life

People will love content that helps them to create, do, or learn something wonderful. It's even better if the post comes in words like 'Do this in a few minutes' or 'How to' or 'Win something' or 'Share this for free gift' or '10 Hacks to.' All these posts contain promising words to attract readers by subtly or overtly telling them that if they read this post, they can learn, buy, win, or create something. In essence, this tactic increases their likelihood of sharing your content.

Do common headlines change depending on social network?

There is a trend regarding how posts are circulated among social media networks. For example, Facebook, YouTube and Google+ are very much home-oriented therefore you would find plenty of 'How-To's,' DIY videos, homemade posts and recipes. Twitter is more business and technology focused, whereas Instagram tends to veer towards lifestyle and fitness.

Common Words/Phrases In Highly-Shared Headlines, By Social Network

Facebook	Twitter	Google+	Pinterest	LinkedIn
things	google	chocolate	chicken	google
recipe	facebook	butter	chocolate	facebook
about	giveaway	recipe	recipe	should
video	about	peanut	butter	social
should	should	google	wedding	about
reasons	social	cream	peanut	chicken
homemade	media	cookies	cookies	things
healthy	reasons	chicken	homemade	apple
every	twitter	cheese	salad	ideas
people	android	cookie	cream	media

= Possible list-posts

= Shows a unique characteristics of this social network

OkDork BY NOAH KAGAN

CoSchedule

Takeaway #4 – List-posts Do Best On Facebook, Twitter, and LinkedIn

We know that list posts are shared quickly and easily but which of these networks work excellently for posts like these?

Using the common terms guide above, it becomes obvious that certain words indicate that list-based posts work excellently on these networks. Words like 'Thing', 'Should' and 'Reasons' feature prominently on Twitter, LinkedIn and Facebook.

Using this information, you can easily think about headlines you've seen on these platforms:

- 10 clever ways to use binder clips

- 5 hacks for better SEO

- 15 places to visit in Colorado

List posts often use highly emotional terms, which is a strong reason why they are shared.

Takeaway #5 – Video Is Most Popular On Facebook

Facebook is by far the most popular platform to feature video content, apart from YouTubr. This is also due to the fact on how Facebook easily allows videos to be embedded into its newsfeed. Taking advantage of this, lately there has been plenty instructional video that is not more than 1 minute long, as seen on things like Tasty or Crafty.

Takeaway #6 – Customize Headlines For Each Social Network

As you know, each social network has its own demographic and its own audience therefore each of this platform should be catered to individually. We realize that Facebook and Pinterest are more home-oriented whereas LinkedIn and Twitter are much more business oriented whereas Snapchat and Instagram are more lifestyle based. Each of these platforms caters to different audiences and therefore they require different types of content.

To accommodate this, writing custom headlines for each social network is essential rather than sharing the same post with the same title for each network. For Twitter, whether you like it or not, you already need to tweak your headlines to fit its 140 character limit. So while this may sound tedious, tweak whenever necessary.

Which platform does the world's most popular headlines get shared?

To understand how shareable headlines work is also to understand how users will ultimately share your content. Here is how users on different social networks share content. As you can see, Pinterest is the leader in sharing and pinning content and why wouldn't it be as the platform was created for the sole purpose of bookmarking things on the internet in the most convenient way possible.

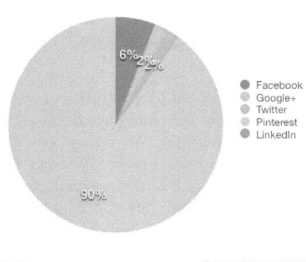

Share Distribution By Social Network

● Facebook
● Google+
● Twitter
● Pinterest
● LinkedIn

Takeaway #7 – Pinterest Offers HUGE Shares If You Can Reach The Audience

Pinterest is huge, but in order to get your post shared on Pinterest, you need the right type of content. Words alone will not cut it. Pinterest thrives on beautiful images as well, just like Instagram's carefully curated, expertly shot mobile pictures. However, creating the right content with the right headline and images will get your post picked up and pinned-plenty of times.

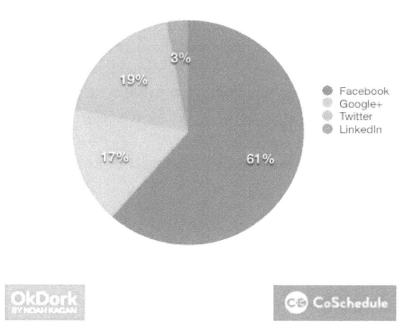

Share Distribution By Social Network w/o Pinterest

Takeaway #8 –Facebook is still the frontrunner

When you remove Pinterest from the equation, you get Facebook coming in second place as the most popular network for shared content. So when it comes to shared content, you want to gain a bigger portion of both Facebook and Pinterest.

Can a marketer predict the popularity of a headline?

Just like there's an app for everything, there is also a web tool for everything. As an online marketer, you need to take advantage of resourceful tools that make your life easier. The same goes to testing headlines to rate them if they are going to be an attention grabber and well-shared post. The Emotional Marketing Value Headline Analyzer was created for this purpose by the Advanced Marketing Institute. This web tool allows a marketer to identify how emotionally driven your headline is by using the number of emotional words used in the phrase as a measurement yardstick.

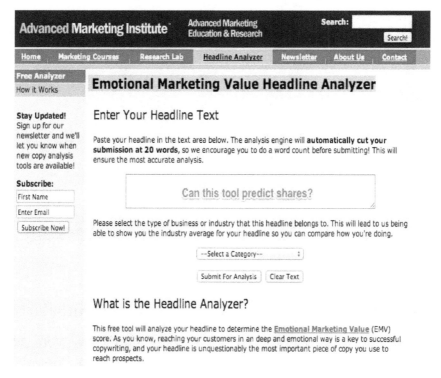

Above is a screenshot of the website. This tool is easy to use as all you need to do is copy and paste your headline into the box, and it'll give you a score of your headline based on the EMV scale.

The analyzer works by rating your headlines according to the emotional marketing value or EMV.

Here were the results:

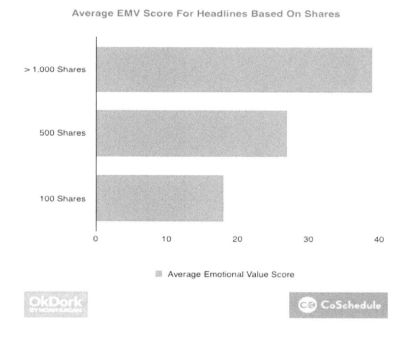

Posts with a high number of shares usually have an EMV Score of 30 or 40, which are several points more than posts with fewer shares.

Takeaway #9 – Emotional Headlines are shared more!

As the numbers of shares increased, the EMV score on a post also increased. There is a direct connection between the quantity of emotional words used and the probability of being shared more than 1,000 times. This is something marketers can enforce for future posts.

Headlines with more emotional words connect to readers even more making them share posts like this faster. CoSchedule also conducted a quick research on the five more shared posts and the five least shared posts on some of the world's most popular blogs to find out with the EMV score would still continue to be a good indicator of sharing probability and here is what they found:

	Avg. EMV Score For Most Popular Posts	Avg. EMV Score For Least Popular Posts
Upworthy.com	33	26
OkDork.com	32	26
Buffer	25	23

The answer is yes. Even the least popular posts earned a pretty good EMV score.

Takeaway #10 – You Can easily measure The Emotional Value Of A Headline

Based on the results above, it looks like every post should be having an EMV headline of at least 30 or above to make it shareable. An EMV of 40 will definitely increase the chances of the post being shared. So if you don't know if your headline is good enough, then use the checker tool to assess. The headlines of a post are the first things a reader will look at, followed by the accompanying photo, so when you create your post or content, make sure the headline correlates with the image poster.

A good way to create good content is to always check the virility of your headline by analyzing the EMV score for your current posts, so that you can create future posts that have a higher value.

Chapter 5- Examples of Affiliate Marketing

In this chapter, we will look at real life examples of successful affiliate marketing endeavors to get you inspired and motivated to build your own site and work on affiliate marketing as a substantial side business.

- **Nerdwallet**

Considered a veteran in the affiliate marketing scene, Nerdwallet has a gold rank if you want to get inspiration. Plenty of marketers will tell you that they favor this affiliate website as the content is genuinely useful and it does exceedingly well in a competitive market. If you want information on financial products and where to get what you are looking for, NerdWallet is your source of information. This is a site you can go to if you need advice, reviews and information on everything financial from insurance to investing, mortgages to credit cards. Their content is stellar, their user-interface is exceptional and they also have a really good marketing team behind them. Nerdwallet is the gold-standard for affiliate marketing sites because they have a niche focus which is finance, they service a consumer niche which are people looking for information on financial products and services, and they also have a goal which is to help these people pick the best option for financial matters. This site currently has 10.6 million visitors a month. Nerdwallet is a 100% affiliate site, there are no ads and they also do not sell their own financial products.

What can you learn from Nerdwallet?

❏ Nerdwallet's most engaging content comes into will form. They give a great user experience and their tools attract plenty of links. SEO plays an integral part of this site.

❏ Nerdwallet also updates their key pages constantly. Their most popular contents are updated annually, making it relevant and enabling their marketing team to market it again.

- **Money Saving Expert**

With a website URL that directly says MoneySavingExpert.com, you're bound to be getting plenty of visits just for your URL alone. This site gives out advice and information to help users make informed financial decisions. They operate the site as a financial education site that explores opportunities for people to get more bang for their buck. Kicked off in 2003, this site was created by Martin Lewis and is currently ranked as one of the most influential affiliate websites for consumers in UK. The site currently amasses 8 million unique visitors a month. MoneySavingExpert sets apart itself from the rest of the pack thanks to quality of content as well as the passion of helping consumers. The goal of this site is to help people make better financial decisions with ethical, accurate and updated financial information. The site is financed by monetizing affiliate links. The monetize their site by using several approaches. Firstly, their use of coupons. MoneySavingsExperts curates a list of deals and coupons for a variety of retailers, making a cut from each sale. Their site also has plenty of 'Best of' guides that feature products and services from banks and credit cards and it takes cut from each sign up from these affiliate links. They also take a cut from their 'Cheap XX' guides that help users choose the cheapest consumer products of a certain category. On the MoneySavingsExperts site, you'll also see a number of calculators from mortgage to loan calculators and each time there is a recommended financial product, MSE gets the cut. MSE also utilizes Amazon discount finders as well as Skimlinks in forum threads.

What can you learn from MoneySavingExpert?

❏ You will see that the MSE website if very well designed and organized. Their articles are also heavily formatted so as to make it as easy as possible to browse.

❏ They also stand out due to their strong editorial code of ethics which identifies correct affiliate links and minimizes any misinformation.

❏ They also maintain 'hero' pages which are highly visual pages that allow readers to get a quick glance of their best options. These hero pages are used-focused and always rank well on search engines.

❏ Each blog post, calculator, content and product has a call-to-action. There is no unnecessary fluff for users to address. Users can immediately go straightforward to the desired information.

- **The WireCutter**

A New York Times Company, the Wire Cutter is a review affiliate website that is a favorite for people looking for gadgets, electronics and related consumer goods. Started by Brian Lam, the former editor of Gizmodo, this site puts all reviewed products through innovative and strenuous tests. Known on the Internet as 'Mythbusters for Gadgets', the WireCutter has grown to become one of the top 6,000 online sites that feature the best products in each of their listed categories. Their product niche is to showcase consumer product reviews and their main goal is to enable people to find the best consumer products in their selected category. Their website currently sees a visitor rate of 3.6 million a month. The Wire Cutter explains clearly how their monetization model works under their 'How to Support Us' page. It is a really simply model that focuses on affiliate commissions through BestBuy and Amazon. Like the MoneySavingExpert and NerdWallet, The Wire Cutter also does not do any sponsored posts or any advertisements; it also does not sell its own products.

To monetize their site, they also have 'Best of' product pages full of product recommendations for each category and this gives Wire Cutter's bulk of profits. For each recommendation, there is an Amazon link and for every affiliate link that is clicked on, Wire Cutter takes a cut. One unique thing about Wire Cutter is that they answer readers' questions constantly, extending the customer service experience and they get a cut from the product sales made. Wire Cutter also uses other reputable retailers, other than Amazon, and they also utilize Skimlinks to make money online. Wire Cutter indicates that there are some forms of advertising, but these details are not readily available.

What can you learn from Wire Cutter?

❑ The Wire Cutter has focus. Instead of creating plenty of new posts on gadgets every month, they focus instead on in-depth reviews.

❑ Their clever use of design makes browsing reviews easy and fast for users.

❑ Their focus is quality and not quantity. Their tests are innovative and extensive tests on products increase their credibility and they live up to their name of testing all products to be the best in their class. Wire Cutter also produces an average of 6 to 12 posts a month.

- **Dating Advice**

The dating scene on the Internet is an extremely lucrative one, but it is also filled with plenty of scam and spam sites that send traffic to other affiliate offers. DatingAdvice.Com sets itself apart from the rest by focusing on a niche. Their site is fun, clean. Their main focus is on expert advice and they emphasize on answering real questions users usually will have. So in essence, their niche is to provide dating advice as well as dating website reviews with the goal to improve people's dating skills and find the best dating sites that fit their needs. Their website amasses a monthly visit of 413 thousand people.

atingAdvice.com makes the bulk of its profits from referring its users to dating websites such as eHarmony and Match.com. All of its recommended sites are mainstream and wholesome. Apart from that, DatingAdvice.com also has its own 'Best of' lists as well as best websites, best apps, products for dating and takes a cut for any sign-ups or sales that have been made. The reviews of popular dating sites also attract plenty of reads and they make money out of the affiliate commissions. As far as revenues go, these two types of content bring in the profits for DatingAdvice.Com. They also have sponsored posts that bring in some money for them.

What can you learn from them?

- ❑ The main thing that DatingAdvice.Com does spectacularly well is to keep their site clean. They keep a healthy, wholesome image without any scams, spams and sexual content. The designs, the colors and the use of faces in practically all posts goes a long way in telling users that this site is safe.

- ❑ Another way they keep it clean is by having no banner ads anywhere on the site. Banner ads have a long history of being spammy and it can also cheapen the design of a site: and for DatingAdvice that has a very cohesive design, it will definitely hurt, especially if you are monetizing your site with affiliates.

- ❑ They also have section for 'As Features in,' which has logos of mainstream, well-known publications. This helps the site establish credibility and sincerity and it also affirms the mainstream nature of the content. This social proof is excellent in maintaining a credible, trustworthy site.

❑ Lastly, DatingAdvice focuses on expert advice. Their advice is not from any random person but instead, features relationship experts as well as dating and marriage counselors. This also adds to the credibility of their site and gives authority.

- **PC Part Picker**

When you look at this website, you'll notice the design itself sets itself apart from traditional affiliate websites. It is not just another content targeting site that has 'the Best of'. Not that best-of listicles are bad- they are great and everyone loves them, but PC Part Picker is on a league of its own because they've managed to build something that provides extreme value that enables the site to market itself. The website's focus is basically as a tool for users who want to build their own computers, with the focus on gaming computers. The difficult part about building computers is getting the right information without browsing too many websites and getting information overload. New computer parts are constantly out in the market and finding the latest ones that fit your budget and needs take time to research. Plus, you will also want to know their compatibility.

What PC Part Picker does is just that- picks all the information apart for you. The site allows you to shop for the latest computer parts based on budget and performance and it also cross-references products to check compatibility. This site operates as a tool but it also has a nice blog that dispenses advice and other information on computers. PC Part Picker has a niche, which are computer parts. They have a goal to help people build computers and they have a website that enables these two elements to come together. The website receives about 3.3 millions visitors on a monthly basis.

PC Part Picker monetizes their site through affiliate links via user-created or expert-created PC builds. They also focus on individual reviews on computer components. In the expert-created PC builds, experts put together a PC for you on the site via a blog post. If users like what they read, they can click on the affiliate links to purchase the component.

Individual component reviews on the other hand use historical price data to help people make better purchasing decisions for their computer parts.

What can you learn from PC Part Picker?

❑ Their site is built as a tool. While they do have a blog and valuable content, their main game is the PC - building tool.

❑ Their main focus is on user experience. Everything from the tools to the parts is geared to help users achieve a specific goal, which is to build a PC that has no compatibility issues and within a certain budget.

❑ They make it easier for users to shop around for the right component. By being a member of various affiliate programs, PC Part Picker can help users to gain the best component at their desired price range and they even go beyond just recommending products on their site- they also help readers to achieve a good shopping experience.

- **50em.com**

This site has just 7 pages. It does not have a well-established team or a large budget. It also lacks existing audiences. 50em's main goal is to help readers choose between two of the most popular automation tools currently on the market which are InfusionSoft as well as Ontraport. These tools represent a huge spend for any marketeer and they also run into hundreds of dollar every month. 50em, by crafting an ultra-focused, hyper-targeted content makes the selection process between these two easier and of course brings in the profit for them. This site is a master-class in creating high-impact, high-value product reviews.

There are plenty of things you can learn from this site. Primarily, they have a focus which is automation software reviews and their main goal is to help marketers choose between Ontraport and InfusionSoft.

Wondering how they make money? The monetization method for 50em is the same like the rest- through affiliate commissions. Both InfusionSoft and Ontraport are expensive, starting from $199 to $297 a month. A single sale is wildly lucrative. To make these commissions, 50em creates in-dept reviews for both Ontraport as well as InfusionSoft. These are texts as well as videos to explain each product well and it gives plenty of value to their readers.

Apart from this, 50em also gives high-quality head-to-head comparisons, if the reviews themselves are not convincing enough for you. You can compare both products against each other, by reading in-depth breakdown of each software's weaknesses as well as strengths.

Users will be able to read recommendations apart from the comparisons and reviews. On the site, there is a self-serve page for recommendations, enabling you to select a product that meets your needs. Last but not least is the 'Ask Me' tool which enables 50em to give their users an option to get direct answers to any queries they have on automation.

What can you learn from 50em?

❏ They selected the right niche. All they ever talk about are just two tools- InfusionSoft and Ontraport and nothing else clutters the site. It's straightforward and hyper-focused. While extremely narrow, this niche brings in high profits even if the sale volume is low.

❏ 50em provides users with first-hand experience through their reviews, comparisons and the Ask Me feature. While there may be plenty of text, you'd find that none of it has fluff but offers value overall.

❏ 50em also invests a lot of time in their copy. Their content is easy to read and fun and not at all boring.

❏ It helps users choose easily and wisely. The recommendations, reviews, and comparisons take a lot of time to write and create, but the outcome makes it easier for readers to choose the right software for their needs.

- **This is why I'm Broke**

  With an extremely quirky name, This is Why I'm Broke is an affiliate marketing space that was among the first affiliate websites to materialize on the internet and their focus is on novelty and gift aggregation angle. This site taps into pop-culture and finds strange and unique gifts that appeal to people's sense of fun, excitement and strange. You can find the unique to the bland on this site, but it generally delivers more exclusive stuff than anything else. It is difficult not to click on any of these affiliate links.

This is why I'm Broke is great because they focus on their product niche, which is novelty items and gifts: and their goal is to source the web to find the weird, the wacky and the unique for people.

As an affiliate site, they make most of their money through affiliate offers, especially through Amazon Associates Program. They also generate their money through selling stuff on Etsy, appearing as an affiliate there. They also do not add links on every page or article, so it does seem that they do not monetize all of their pages.

What can you learn from This is Why I'm Broke?

❏ They have the fun factor, which is a natural marketing. This is does not do active marketing but it does attract its fair share of people coming in from natural links and shares on their posts. This is mainly due to the fun factor in their articles.

❏ The fact that they do not monetize all their content is a source of credibility and authenticity, keeping in line with the fun factor of the site. Some posts are just for fun which provides a great user experience and goes a long way in terms of boosting the site's reputation and credibility.

- **Making Sense of Cents**

This is another financial matter site that was created and run by Michelle Gardner. This is not so much of a big finance site like the others on this chapter. Making Sense of Cents is written entirely by Michelle which makes the advice on the site more personal, rather than advice coming from a team of experts. Using her own writing in the content has paid off for her big-time. Michelle publishes her income reports on the blog and the last one showed an income revenue of $125,000. In terms of an individual blogger doing well with affiliate marketing, Michelle has proven that you can get all the way up there. Her niche is personal and family finance, and her goal is to help people budget and save money.

Of course she makes money through a variety of affiliate marketing as well as selling her own courses. She also earns money through advertising on her blog but the main revenue comes from Affiliate Marketing.

What can you Learn from Making Sense of Cents?

❑ Firstly, by taking a personal angle, this blog differentiated itself from other competitive content blogs. Finance is a hyper-competitive market and Michelle can compete by making her content and style personable.

❑ She has her readers' backs. Plenty of Michelle's top content enables her readers to earn a little bit of money through saving and budgeting effectively. It is not about reviewing products but more about helping people.

- **The Points Guy**

The travel and finance avenues make up some of the biggest affiliate sites to date. The Points Guy focuses on social traffic which rakes in plenty of organic traffic via social sites. Their niche is the use of credit cards for travel purposes and teaching people how they can benefit from the use of credit cards for getting better service, or free fares or travel luxuriously on a cheap budget. The Points Guy is extremely popular, thanks to its super-focus on helping people do extremely specific things- which is to get stuff for free!

This site is a master-class in combining solving a problem and recommending products to earn an affiliate commission. Their niche is credit cards and travel and their goal is travel and credit card hacking. The affiliate program of credit cards and travel is how The Points Guy makes money. Their focus is directly on people using credit cards to earn travel rewards.

What can we learn from The Points Guy?

❑ Solve a problem with your site. Just because you are an affiliate does not mean you can blindly write about products and services that you do not believe in. Take a focus and actually help people solve their problems and you'd enjoy free marketing and ever-growing popularity thanks to your genuine output, the desire to help as well as producing content that is valuable.

❑ Place your best products in the limelight just like the Points Guy has a 'Top Cards' Section that lists top travel credit cards. It does not bring as much traffic as some other content, but it definitely helps. It gives people an easy place to find the most valuable products for people specifically looking for this type of information.

- **Just A Girl And Her Blog**

This blog is your cut and paste affiliate website- this blog uses Amazon Associates program to sell things about crafts or organization or anything related to DIY. Immensely popular, this blog has enabled her to earn at least $40k a month through affiliate marketing. Her blog works because of the niche- organizing and DIY and her goal is to help people organize, simplify and beautify their lives. Abby makes her money through Amazon Affiliates and it is also hosted using BlueHost. Another way she makes her income is by selling courses related to her niche.

What can we learn from Just a Girl and Her Blog?

❏ Her blog is a like a guinea pig. She tries various things and details her experiences, so her readers do not have to go through the process of testing things on their own. She eliminates this problem. She also recommends products she believes in along the way.

❏ Social media is a big useful tool for blogs. If you are in a niche that works well in social media, then you need to utilize them.

Bottom Line

The sites listed here is just a handful of the best practices and examples on the internet where affiliate marketing is concerned. All of these blogs and sites have one thing in common- an invest of time in quality content and the need to address a specific problem. Your involvement in the affiliate marketing channel you choose is entirely up to you, but it also depends on the product or niche you have chosen on the kind of income you get. If you want positive outcomes, then invest in good content, time and a good site.

Chapter 6- How to Achieve $10,000 a month through Affiliate Marketing

We all have aspirations of making it big, or at least making our ventures successful. We all want things to work out for the best, and we all want to get profits with whatever endeavors we invest, so it is not a surprise if we think about hitting that golden $10k in revenue through affiliate marketing.

Affiliate marketing takes a good investment in time to make it sustainable and credible. Plenty of good and positive stories are around to make good money with affiliate marketing, but what can you do as a beginner? Can you actually hit $10k?

The immediate answer is a resounding YES. If you know how the basic function of affiliate marketing works, how to use the Internet and the basic requirement of a computer-you are already one step ahead of the pack to start making money with affiliate marketing.

In this chapter, we will investigate the things you can do to ensure you get profit. Keep in mind that this is not a one-size-fits-all template. Affiliate marketing also depends on your tenacity to market your site as effectively as possible.

You can achieve 10k a month by doing very simple things on your site.

But first, answers these questions:

1- Have you selected your niche?

2- Have you identified what problem you are solving with your niche?

3- Have you chosen a program or network to join?

4- Have you optimized your blog/site to fit your needs and your niche?

Once you have all your bases covered, let us look into deeper details to help you stay at the top of your game:

- Stay Ethical, Keep things legal

It is important to protect yourself. Depending on where your business is located, you are bound by terms and conditions and legal issues related to affiliate marketing. In the US for example, you need to disclose that your link is an affiliate link. The affiliate disclosure must be part of the link or as close as possible to the link itself and not at the bottom of your posts. Failure to disclose is an accident waiting to happen and whatever you have earned may end up going for legal fees if you do not do your business ethically and legally. It may seem tedious, but it will save you time and money in the long run.

- Cloak your links

Most affiliate links are very messy with all sorts of numbers and words. As an affiliate, you want to create links that are not confusing and also easily searchable on search engines. Getting custom urls for your products or cloaking them helps you gain visibility and credibility as well. Use <u>Pretty Link Lite</u> to cloak your affiliate links. It's free to use and once you've done so, it is easily to find your affiliate links and also, with cloaked links, your content is less spammy. People will trust your domain and are more likely to click through your links.

- Recommend things you will use yourself

You'd have more passion to continue what you are doing and promote what you love only if you believe in the product. Genuine love and enthusiasm is what will get you more and more people coming to your site. You cannot fake this for a long period of time- maybe for a short time but what happens when you run out of ideas of content? Promoting a product/service that you genuinely like will help you get more of the product- what are its benefits, its pain points, what the audience is saying and so on. You want to make more and more ethical decisions as your business grows and promoting something you know and use will help you make better decisions in your business to increase profits.

Knowing your products and giving your feedback and review will bring you more fans. When brands notice this, they will be more willing to give you a higher cut for every sale. You may have two products that you need to review and both has its fair share of advantages, but you have a better understanding of a product and its best features, so you may want to recommend that on a genuine point of view compared to another product.

- Expertly weave in your links

When you do affiliate marketing, you have a choice of your involvement because your involvement determines your profits. Do you want to go all out and provide excellent, quality content in return for high profits or do you want average or low involvement which also translates to low profits? This choice is yours, but when you do promote products and services, you want to masterfully recommend these products in a way that is non-spammy. When you provide content that is not spammy, your users are more likely to believe you and trust what you are saying.

When you deliver content that is helpful, they are more likely to share your content because they have found value in the content and they believe others will to. So when you use affiliate links, make sure to weave them in as naturally as possible. It's all about context. Put yourself in your user's shoes and look at your content- is it something you would read yourself?

If you want to make money with affiliate marketing, content and context is key. The affiliate links you use must make sense in your post. Randomly dropping them in your content is not very helpful

- Add affiliate links to your popular posts

As we discovered from 50em or even WireCutter in the previous chapter, updating content and marketing them is one way of staying fresh. You can freshen up your posts but updating them with affiliate links and adding new content in them.

Keep in mind NOT to over-link your post though. You can also try linking your top-converting blog posts with affiliate links. Tutorial posts, best of's and cheapest kind of posts really work in this avenue. You do not need to make complex articles just to add links- updating what you have sometimes goes a long way.

- Resource Pages

Your resource page gives you a wealth of links. You want to create a resource page that lists all the products you recommend. Say for example if you are a makeup blogger, then there can be a page full of makeup products you love. You can even make a list of makeup products that are vegan and cruelty free or best makeup for skin color or best makeup for travelling. Get the idea? There are plenty of ways you can add your link and the resource page denotes one of them.

- Target audience

One of the best ways to make sure you get profits and reach your 10k target is to make sure your target audience and your niche are aligned. What are you promoting? To Whom are you promoting it to? What problems are you solving for them? One reason why you may not get the kind of money you want through affiliate marketing is the misaligned audience and niche. You are probably recommending a product your target audience does not need. Say for instance you are a vegan blogger. What would your main source of income come from? It wouldn't be on kitchen gadgets would it? It would probably be on recommendation on vegan food guides, vegan travel tips, vegan restaurants, and vegan products.

This is because your target audience is just like you- people who are foodies but want vegan alternatives. To be successful in affiliate marketing is to keep your audience needs in mind. Always think- how am i solving my audience's problems today?

- Experiment with different styles

Affiliate links come in many different formats and styles. You do not want to stick to just one even if they yield the most traffic for you. You want to diversify so you can reach a wider audience. Use product images, simple links, coupon and discount codes as well as cleverly placed banner ads. You also want to play around with your content format and recommend products in different ways from lists to photos, stories and video. You may want to choose both formats (write up and video) if your product needs it.

- Newsletters

Some people prefer reading long-format articles right from their inbox or they prefer getting notifications of your new post from their inbox. This is where you can include your affiliate links into your email campaigns. Add in your affiliate links where appropriate into your newsletter. You can also send out newsletters on affiliate products that you love but make sure to include them in a good way such as in an email challenge or a social media giveaway. We all know how hard it is to build an email list and get active subscribers so do not let this go to waste. Use your email marketing as best as you can.

- Lead Magnet

Another way to ensure you get your 10k mark in terms of profit is to add your affiliate links to freebies or lead magnets. Lead magnets have been proven to be extremely effective for all age groups. You can definitely bet that your audience, or at least a majority of them would be consuming your lead magnet and when it is relevant, weave in your best affiliate links in them.

These tips are all great ways to ensure that you content and context is sustainable. You need to do these things in order to make your site visible and credible, so you will have a continuous stream of audience coming in from all corners of the Internet. Always make sure to try and test different formats, links and such so you will know what works and what does not.

Making your $10,000 Sustainable

- Scaling Your Business

In order to reach your goal of $ 10,000 revenue in your affiliate marketing business, one needs to know when the time is right to scale your business. Only by doing so can you be able to generate a larger revenue that meets your business goals at the end of the day. The best way to grow your drop shipping business is to relook back into the ads that are performing well.

Redirect a portion of your profits into those ads to capitalize on the ads performance to your intended customer pool. Reinvesting the profits back into your business will ensure that you keep your money rolling within it in order to make it more successful in the long run. In the start, it is usually the norm that business owners do not take a salary (maybe in the first year or two). They keep channeling their profits into the business to grow it further until it becomes more sustainable and competitive.

- Outsourcing

For any new business that is starting from the ground up, it becomes vital to be economical as possible. This is to ensure that funds and profits are first and foremost invested back into the business to generate growth, be competitive and increase revenue.

Once you've scaled your business and the revenue stream is sustainable and growing, you will need to start looking into the possibilities of hiring extra hands to manage the business. This is because time is limited and there aren't enough hours in day to accomplish all tasks relevant to your business. Hence, outsourcing or adding on manpower into your business is one way to ensure the business operations run smoothly and you will be able to focus your energy into growing the business and generating revenue.

- Growing Your Business Using Data

In any business, be it the traditional or online method, data is vital in growing the business in order to stay relevant and to stay ahead of the competition. Using Google Analytics and Facebook conversion pixel data, you will be able to track every single data to grow your business. You will be able to know specific details of your customer, for example their locality and the path they took to your website which generated the sale in the end. This will in turn allow you to determine what works and what doesn't work on your website to enable a farther reach to a larger pool of customers.

Chapter 7- Tips to Becoming a Successful Affiliate Marketer

What does it take to become a successful affiliate?

It's always hard for me to come up with an answer.

However, I always try to devise some sort of plan for an answer.

So here are the steps to become successful in affiliate marketing!

Selecting The Right Merchants

As an affiliate marketer, it is not a priority at the start to select a merchant that pays the highest commission but it is more important to select one that has a reputable product and a good and stable reputation. Another factor that should be considered is to differentiate the merchants between their sell-through rate.

Importance Of Integrity

When you start to promote a product or service, its always important to note that, never ever sell something that you wouldn't buy for yourself. It doesn't matter which type of channel you use to sell your brand, be it via a website, social media platform, email or a blog, you don't want to promote and sell something that you wouldn't buy for yourself or recommend to your friends or family members. You should be selective on this as carrying a lousy product will only do more harm to your name and business.

Being Niche

The best way to generate income through affiliate marketing is to get more people to visit your website or online store. The more people, the likelihood of more sales is much higher. It is okay to have some competition with other brands or affiliate marketers but you don't want to take on a product or service that already has a saturated market. The key here is to identify a brand that is niche and only serves a particular market segment. But be careful of this as, some brands may not have any competition and that can be an alarm bell as having no competition means that this particular product or service isn't highly sought after by the community.

Being Brand Relevant

To ensure success in affiliate marketing, it is important to ensure that the content on your site and the brand you are promoting are relevant to each other. You cannot promote healthy based foods but have affiliate links and banners on your site promoting fast foods and pizza. These two key areas should be relevant and tie into each other in order to attract and convert potential customers.

Do Not Overcrowd

It's vital that the content on your page is not overshadowed by over excessive banners. Having rows and rows of banners will tend to push potential customers away from your site, and it makes your page look less attractive.

Personal Recommendation

To achieve better sales results, it's best to make a personal recommendation on brands, products and services that you have tried yourself and completely endorse.

Monitor Results

Being a successful affiliate marketer means having a good relationship with your merchant. In order to achieve that you need to have a merchant that has a good track record and is performing. If you affiliate with a merchant that cannot deliver, you are bound to receive many complaints from your customers and drive your business downwards. As such, it is critical to partner with a merchant that has a good track record to ensure your business keeps growing.

Work With Multiple Merchants

In any investment, the main advice you hear is never to put all your eggs in one basket. The same holds true for affiliate marketing. You should not just work with one merchant, but focus on diversifying and having multiple agents have the same item or different items.

Original Content Creation

Having original content is important to an affiliate marketer as Google constantly looks for websites with duplicate content. While you can source the Internet for free content, if your blog or website is identical to others, Google will indefinitely penalize you. As such, always try to be creative and original with your content.

Changing Content

For a new site or blog, you will have immediate traffic once it's up but it will start to dwindle down over time. This is because Google will visit your site; and if there are no new changes, it will start to rank your site lower every time. Therefore, changing and updating your content is important for search engines to rank your platform higher.

Choose Good Products

When starting out as an affiliate marketer, never try to register with many affiliate programs. Since you will be new in this, it can get very overwhelming very fast if you try to promote more than you can. So, you need to carefully select your products and try to understand the market needs and also pick brands that you understand and identify with thoroughly.

Use Many Traffic Sources to Promote Products

Apart from using just ads on your blog or website, you may also opt to use other traffic sources to assist you in promoting your products. With more traffic to your page, you can expect more generation of revenue in the long run. One such tool that can be of use is Google Adwords. It can be used to direct traffic to your webpage. All you need to do is to make an ad using your Adwords account and link it using your affiliate link to the target URL page of the ad.

Learn About the Product And Service You Are Promoting

Always research and learn about the product and service that you will be promoting and selling on your blog or website. Acquire its benefits and disadvantages and what makes it stand out against other brands.

Understand its features, and how it can benefit the user. It is also key to understand the market and the customer demographics that you intend to sell it to. Never carry or promote a product that you lack knowledge of or have never personally used.

Create A Strong Brand Name For Your Niche

As an affiliate marketer, don't just stop after building a one-page campaign. You will also need to work on building assets, funnels and any things that add value to your business. Focus on one particular niche and master it. If you keep doing this, you not only ear your visitor's trust but also open the doors to work with exclusive advertisers to stay ahead of your competitors.

Have A Plan

When starting any business, it is always important to have a plan. Before promoting any product, put yourself in the shoes of the owner. Look from their viewpoint. If you owned that offer, what would you do differently and why? This is particularly important in choosing the right merchant, the right product the right ad campaign and soon on. One tool you can use is to emphasis the usage of the 5Ws, which are the What, Who, Where, When and Why.

The Learning Process Will Take Time

Never expect to make a quick buck out of affiliate marketing in your first few months. As with every learning process in life, things take time. Likewise, you will need to take baby steps in your journey as an affiliate marketer. You need to understand your product and services, the market space, your customers, managing websites and ad campaigns. All these take time and can be from a few weeks to months or years before you are successful.

Failure Is Your Friend

Failures are a part of business and you will encounter moments of ups and downs in affiliate marketing. However, failures always teach us a lesson and we should always rise up from each situation instead of quitting. Try to figure out what went wrong and correct your mistakes. Never ever give up and always try something new and be consistent with it and a solution will surely present itself for every problem that arises.

Developing a Positive Attitude in Business

Today, positive thinking is applied in many different fields from business to sales, marketing to advertising, health, sports, education, motivation, inspiration, national allegiance, psychology as well as self-image. Many of the twenty-first-century authors apply positive thinking in various areas. Some of these famous ones are:

Anthony Robbins' seminar and speeches using the knowledge of psychology and positive thinking. Robbins' is a motivational speaker and advisor to many world leaders and have helped ordinary people to achieve success or lead more positive, and fulfilling lives.

Steven Covey is the author of *The 7 Habits of Highly Effective People*, and his points are regularly quotes in businesses and personal development. These seven habits can be used above and beyond the business realm, applying it to almost anything in life.

Louise Hay is the author of *You can Heal Your Life* and several other motivational and self-improvement books. She promotes the use of self-healing to use the power of our thoughts to enhance our lives.

Wayne W. Dyer employs the teaching of Tao Te Ching of Change your thoughts, change your life which directly influences use to lead and live a more balanced and fulfilling lifestyle. Dryer is the author of *The Power of Intention*.

Why Positive Thinking is important for one to truly live and abundant and productive life

How many times have you failed at something and someone- a friend, teacher, classmate, parent, or partner tells you not to give up and focus on the positive?

Sometimes you think that advice is easier said than done. The truth is, focusing our mind on being and thinking positively is fairly straightforward- it is all about controlling your thoughts because of the understanding that a positive attitude leads to a fruitful, and happy life is already a high motivation to change. Having a positive outlook on life will enable you to cope much easily to the affairs of the everyday life from the moment you wake up until the time you go to sleep. A positive outlook gives you an optimistic approach and makes you worry less and think less negative thoughts. It will further enable you to experience the silver lining in the darkest of situations.

A positive mind is a state of mind that is worth developing because everyone can benefit from it and who knows where it will take you?

A positive attitude is noticeable in the following ways:

- Optimistic thinking.
- Constructive thinking.
- Creative thinking.
- Optimism.
- Drive and energy to do things, accomplish goals.
- An attitude of happiness.

A positive mindset can help you in many ways:

- Expecting success as failure is not an option
- The feeling of inspiration in everything you do
- Gives you strength to keep going and not give up
- Helps you overcome obstacles you face
- Gives you the ability to look at failures, mistakes and problems as a blessing in disguise.
- Keeps you believing in yourself, your abilities, and your talents
- Radiate self-esteem and confidence
- You look for solutions instead of dwelling on problems; you seek opportunities when it comes

Positive thinking is a game changer- you can transform your whole life if you always look on the bright side of life instead of wallowing in self-pity and allowing yourself to think negatively. Positive thinking is infectious! It not only affects you but each individual around you- people want to be with you and make friends with you and hang out with you because you've got the drive and energy and positivity, making it so easy to be your friend. You will end up changing the life of those around you, uplifting them and encouraging them to become the best version of themselves. Positivity is a strong emotion, so if you are positive, then you radiate positivity!

Even more benefits of a Positive Attitude:

- You achieve more of your goals easily
- You achieve success much rapidly
- You bring in more happiness in your life and those around you
- You have more energy to deal with everything life throws at you
- You have more faith in your abilities and have higher hopes for a brighter future
- You can inspire and motivate everyone around you
- You feel you encounter fewer obstacles and difficulties compared to other people
- You are much more respected and loved by all those around you
- Life smiles at you

The bottom line is, if you exhibit a negative attitude, then you will only bring in more failure and more difficulties. However, if you radiate positivity, you are bound to be attracting good energy and success so the time is NOW to change the way you think and the way you react.

Negative thoughts, behaviors and reactions do nobody any good. If you have tried to become positive in the past but you have failed, then you have likely not tried enough.

Chapter 8- Top Affiliate Marketing Trends of 2019

Content

In the coming years, content will play an even more important role in affiliate marketing. It won't just come down to what you put up but how it engages your target market. As such, the content has to be not only creative but also eye catching as well. It will also have to incorporate both audio and visual tools that appeals to the target market but will also need to be relevant the search engines as well. As such, you will have to employ various tools such as video demos, pictures and even slideshows to be a step ahead of the competition. However, traditional approaches to content should not be pushed aside and forgotten, as these tools are still needed to provide the necessary information and descriptions.

Affiliate Marketing Discounts

In 2016, the U.S Department of Industrial Policy and Promotion (DIPP) introduced a ban to online platforms in offering discounts. As such, these platforms could not offer the utilization of cash to give huge discounts or subsidize certain products. Since this ban was introduced, online marketplaces started to look at affiliate marketing as an option to provide indirect discounting. Top affiliate marketing websites generate their revenue by increasing traffic into their online stores. A commission is then charged and directed back towards the website. It is through this commission that customers can enjoy benefits like in the form of discounts and cashbacks. This has shown to be a huge appeal to customers looking for good deals on products and services online.

Use of Artificial Intelligence

The usage of artificial intelligence is quickly becoming a useful and important tool in affiliate marketing. The technology is often used by affiliate marketing to ensure smooth communication and also to help in monitoring performance. One example of this is IBM Watson and WebGains, an affiliate marketing platform came together to create its first chatbot. It is evident that within the next few years and with the improvements in technology, we will be seeing this tool becoming more effective for affiliate marketers.

The Use of Voice Search

The use of voice searches has increased exponentially ever since tools such as Google Home and Siri have entered the market. As such, Internet searches are moving more towards voice searches and affiliate marketers will need to invest more time and money into optimizing voice searches. Converting from normal search engine optimization (SEO) methods is easier said than done. As such, developers will need to look at all possible avenues such as natural languages and long keywords that are more likely be used in voice searches. Big names such as Apple, Amazon, Google and even Facebook have already jumped on the voice search bandwagon, and other players will soon follow suit.

The Use of Influencers

With the huge rise of social media platforms like Facebook, Instagram and Youtube, it has also given birth to a new trend of social media influencers. These influencers use their popularity to market products and service to generate income. An influencer is an individual who has a huge popularity or followers that listen or emulate them. They collaborate with marketers to promote products, services and even events to their followers. Apart from that, links can be placed in these influencers bio or comments sections to channel traffic to the specific website that they are promoting. As such, it has become the latest trend for the younger generation. This has pushed many ad agencies to increase their budget on social media influencer marketing to catch this trend.

Mobile Phones Market Is Growing

In a recent 2018 survey, research revealed that the mobile phones made up of 61% of all online views as compared to 52% in 2015. In developing countries especially in Asia, growth is more profound due to the influx of new mobile brands such as Oppo and Huawei that are challenging for the market space. As such, affiliate marketers will need to ensure that they construct their webpages as mobile-friendly to users and also prevent any clickloss when traffic is directed to their webpages.

Use of Keyword-Rich Reviews

Another important trend involves product reviews that are keyword-rich. This is particularly important when customers are reading through testimonials, which indicates that they are one step away from getting a purchase. To help make this push from search to purchase, high-quality and honest reviews are needed from the affiliate marketers. And as an affiliate marketer, it is vital that you provide good content and also ensure that all the reviews are real and honest. It is also imperative that you work with individuals who are interested in posting reviews of your products and services.

Native Advertising

Some of the challenges advertisers face is customers not being attracted to banners on websites. Moreover, publishers have moved towards creating valuable content using native advertising. Using native advertising, affiliate marketers can focus on sharing information in a way that is more attractive to the visitors to the website. Native advertising can also be utilized for directing traffic to your website and also for content promotion.

GDPR Aftermath, Privacy, and Data

The General Data Protection Regulation or GDPR is a regulation on an individual's personal data that came into the picture in mid-2018 and has had an impact on affiliate marketing. When this regulation came into play, many types of campaigns and tactics became redundant overnight and caused affiliate marketers to rethink their strategies. With the growing awareness of privacy data, you as an affiliate marketer will need to ensure that your website won't increase your visitor's privacy fears. For this reason, a Secure Sockets Layer or SSL needs to be used to create an environment where potential customers feel safe when making purchases and sharing their personal data.

Anti-Fraud Tools

In 2018, it was estimated that about $19 billion was wasted online due to ad fraud and Pixalate is estimating that it will make up about 17% of online traffic in 2019. As an affiliate marketer, this can be negated by analyzing bot behavior and monitoring patterns from data. Also, to battle ad fraud, make sure any traffic source or tracker that you choose is well-equipped to battle ad fraud.

Emails For Affiliate Marketing

Many affiliate marketers have their own lead list used to market and communicate with their customers that will be interested in their products and services. There are many types of lead lists that these affiliate marketers integrate. The first one that is commonly used is the list containing regular visitors of the affiliate marketer's website. These visitors enjoy the content that the affiliate marketers deliver and they are more likely to make a purchase when they receive email notifications on a product update or review. The next type is when business owners or companies share their lead list with affiliate marketers for their promoted products and services.

As an affiliate marketer, when receiving these leads, it's best to classify them into segments to make sure you are getting high quality leads from the business owners to make this work. Always bear in mind that the end game is create ad campaigns that attract potential customers and convert them into making purchases. The better and higher quality leads will lead to higher chances of making a sale. Many business owners predict that the trend of using email for affiliate marketing will continue to grow and evolve into better ad campaigns to target specific customer markets.

Live Streaming And Interactive Ads

The use of live streaming and interactive ads can also help to direct traffic and potential customers to your website. By employing various incentives, affiliate marketers can makeshift offers when conducting live streaming demonstrations. A couple of segments that are useful for this are the fitness and personal care industry. Potential customers can purchase these products by going to the weblinks that appear during these live streaming demonstrations.

Smaller Networks Will Get More Attention

It is predicted that in 2019, many smaller affiliate marketing websites may start giving larger platforms a run for their money. While these smaller networks lack the marketing and presence as opposed to the well-established affiliate marketing websites, their strength will come from the fact that they serve a specific group of customers with very niche products and services.

The Rise of SaaS Products

Software as a Service or called SaaS for short is the process of marketing software and applications to companies and individuals that require them. This application still hasn't really caught up with affiliate marketers, as it's quite hard to market. But many affiliate marketers are beginning to use this app in 2019, so it's becoming more popular.

Affiliate Diversification

Previously, many business owners targeted their focus on at least one or two affiliate companies that already had a wide array of products and services. In keeping with changing times, these methods are proving far less fruitful and currently there is a change by these business owners to diversify their pool of affiliate marketers. Business owners are now targeting smaller, niche affiliate marketers in order to market their products and services.

Working With Agencies

Another rising trend in 2019 for affiliate marketers reflects the use of influencer marketing agencies. These agencies are the ones that are responsible for connecting influencers and bloggers with the products and services. These agencies will source for products and services that influencers are interested in and also identify influencers for their customers.

Experts (Individuals) of Affiliate Marketing

Brian Marcus, VP Global Marketing at TUNE, says that with an advertiser's need to increase growth and engage more customers, one will start to venture into more mobile-savvy performance-based partnerships. For affiliate marketing, there is also a large untapped market in e-commerce, travel and finance industry. He also states that new innovations in marketing will rise from mobile-online partnerships as customers can experience new and cross-channel offers with just a click of the button.

Kevin Edwards, Global Client Strategy Director of Awin, further contends that affiliate marketers must create a safe online environment for their customers, so that they will be comfortable making purchases and sharing personal data online. This is in wake of the numerous data and privacy breaches that have happened prior to this.

Todd Crawford, VP Strategic Initiatives from Impact, also suggests that partner marketing will take a step forward in 2019 and onwards. He infers that partner marketing has begun to mature and has expanded; he asserts how more brands are moving towards this trend to grow their business.

Julie Van Ullen, GM of Growth for Rakuten Marketing, goes on to say that ad tech companies will need to focus their energies to create an enjoyable customer experience, which will also enable them to serve their publishers and

advertisers in 2019. Some other trends that she also sees are:
-

- Transparency – websites that place priority on transparency in performance and data will create a winning working relationship between publishers and brands.

- Data Driven – a meaningful customer experience can only be created when data is used correctly to target customers and build attractive ad campaigns.

- Artificial Intelligence – the use of this tool is so important to manage the affiliate business

Choots Humphries, Co-President & Owner at LinkConnector, expects that compliance will play an important role for affiliate marketing in 2019. As the industry starts to mature and compete with other areas of marketing, compliance will play an integral role between business owners and affiliate marketers.

Scott Kalbach, Founder & CEO from AvantLink, notices that there will be a significant increase in sales authentic publishers. It used to be coupons, deals, and loyalty sites that dominated the market space for the last several years, but a strong presence of content publishers are slowly making their mark in the arena.

David Naffziger, the CEO from BrandVerity, expects to see the following trends in 2019:

- Increasing awareness of compliance in affiliate marketers – affiliate marketers are taking more responsibility to ensure their partners comply with the policies of their advertisers.

- Increased privacy regulations – With the implementation of the GDPR in EU countries, affiliate marketers in the U.S are also striving to ensure they keep up with the regulation to create a safe environment for their global customers.

Swim Song, Director of Traffic Operation for Mobvista says that focus for affiliate marketers should be turned towards the consumer. As such, he stresses that attention should be made towards mobile content such as games and e-commerce products that suits the individual's daily needs and lifestyle. He also thinks that advertisers will prefer platforms such as Cost Per Sale (CPS) and Cost Per Lead (CPL) as it is a simpler pricing model.

Beatriz Gonzalez, Business Development for Toro Advertising, suggests that e-commerce will play an important role in affiliate marketing as it already represents 10% of total retail sales in the US and it expected to grow up to 15% every year.

Emanuel Cinca, CEO of WHAT THE AFF, also identifies his money of e-commerce as an important trend for affiliate marketing in 2019. He says that both brand owners and affiliate marketers will start investing more into e-commerce to increase the success potential of their respective businesses. He also suggests that in building an e-commerce store, working together with influencers will also be critical due to the huge following they have.

Ada Pizzaro, Digital Marketer for Mobsuite, sees a more direct relationship between the advertiser and the source in 2019. These relationships will allow them to create more exclusive deals and also build trust within one another. She also predicts that 2019 will bring a new light into online shops, native advertising and increased social media presence.

Michael Xu, Founder and CEO of WebEye – envisions a more in depth focus into the use of artificial intelligence to create better ads for both publishers and advertisers. He also estimates it being used in fighting against ad fraud, estimating customers' interests and analyzing data collected. He also sees an overspill of the GDPR compliance effect altering the affiliate marketing landscape. Data and privacy matters will take an importance as affiliate marketers try to dispel the doubts customers have regarding the security of their transactions and data over the Internet.

Adam Esman, Business Development at Evertrack.io, feels that regulations in privacy will continue to increase and gain momentum in 2019. Thus, it will affect the way data is mined and used for advertisers and affiliate marketers alike. He also states that he is starting to see affiliate marketers becoming more open to the use of technology to track and optimize the performance of their business.

Chapter 9 - Tools to Help you in Affiliate Marketing

Tools help you make the best of your time and effort when it comes to marketing. In this chapter, we will look at the tools to help you make full use of your time, efficiently market your site and promote, your affiliations online. Most tools listed here give you a free version (with limited capabilities) or a trial version before requiring you to purchase the full license to use.

If you feel like this tool has met your needs, then sign up for a full package.

- Flippa

This essential tool can help you get into the process of building a sustainable and successful affiliate site from scratch. This site is created as a bidding marketplace for people to buy and sell websites. For affiliate marketers especially, you get to buy sites that already come with strong backlinks and an optimized SEO growth. Keep in mind that you need to conduct a full backlink audit before you purchase a domain from Flippa to ensure that the domain isn't inflated by unethical SEO practices.

- CJ Affiliate

Affiliate marketing begins with a strong partnerships with sites that are in need of sales. CJ Affiliates is a number one resource for affiliate partnerships as it connects affiliates with merchants wanting to drive up sales for their products. Affiliates get paid for each phone call, or lead, or website when visitors peruse a merchant's site from the affiliate links discovered. CJ Affiliate is a great starting point if you want to seek partnerships.

- SEMRush

If you are looking for keyword research, competition analysis and even fixing SEO errors then SEMRush is a tool needed in your affiliate marketing arsenal. This tool is a favorite among marketers who want to understand what kind or type of content drives the highest ROI for their competitors as well as analyze on-page SEO issues. SEMRush is great for finding top performing content from competitors that you should be writing about too, monitoring keyword rankings weekly, and running SEO audits to watch for issues on your website that could potentially hurt your SEO rankings. What's more, you can use SEMRush to monitor press mentions.

- Ahrefs

Ahrefs is another keyword research tool that you can use just like SEMRush. It also provides on-page audits and competitive content analysis. What's different with Ahrefs is that it places a deeper emphasis on backlinks than on-page SEO. Ahrefs gives marketers insights about lost as well as new backlinks as well as sites that are linked to broken pages on your site. Marketers will find it useful to use Ahrefs for reviewing new and lost backlinks, assessing competitor link profiles, and also obtaining new link building opportunities.

You can also use Ahrefs to find sites that are linked to broken pages and of course finding top-performing competitor content. You can try out both SEMRush as well as Ahref's to build on your SEO optimization. If you can invest in both-great but if you cannot then think about what you really want to track first. If you are an industry leader in your niche, SEMRush would prove to be worthwhile. Since both SEMRush and Ahref have trial periods for their software, you can use both and see which works best for you.

- Yoast SEO

Yoast SEO gives you advanced SEO functionality in each and every page which includes the title tag and meta description which you can customize, canonical link customization, sitemap customization as well as meta robots customization. Yoast is a free tool; but if you want 24/7 support, then you can go for the paid version. They also have a redirect manager in the paid version that allows you to redirect broken pages or pages that you want to be removed from search results.

- Grammarly

This example exemplifies another useful tool to have if you are publishing content on a regular basis. It is good to have a tool that can check your spelling, grammar as well as plagiarism all in one go. Grammarly is a master-class tool in spell-check and grammar. It sports incorrect word use as well as comma usage. All in all, it makes your written content even better.

- Duplichecker

If you are part of the content team for your website, then running your article through Duplichecker will help you spot any kind of plagiarism. Of course Grammarly also does this task, but if your intention is only to check plagiarism, then Duplichecker is a good investment tool. Accidental cases of plagiarism can prove to be a painful legal issue, so it's best to get your content checked.

- Hemingway

Another amazing content review tool, Hemingway, helps you to simplify your writing. It is based off the writing style of Ernest Hemingway, hence the name of the software. Whatever content you write, especially the ones that go on the Internet, needs to be simple, straightforward and easy to understand. Your readers what the point to come across fast and their want insights, which means you do not want fluff tossed into your content just to make your sound intelligent. With the Hemingway software, you can simplify complex sentence, and it also points out complex words and adverbs that you can replace with simple ones.

- Sumo

One of the main things you want your site to do is attract visitors and with Suno, you turn your visitors into customers. Most website visitors are not ready to open their wallets and make a purchase with their credit cards when they reach your site, especially if it is their first time visiting. How can you possible get money from them? You sell them things that they are ready to buy. The best way most successful affiliate marketers do is to scale to build their email list. This enables marketers to drive repeat visitors back to their site and also to purchase products over a period of time. With Sumo, you can have easy to install email capture forms on your site.

- Google Adsense

Earning money for each referral you get is wonderful isn't it? Want to elevate this experience? Use Google Adsense! With Google AdSense, you get a second revenue stream as you continue to scale your business. AdSense basically allows you to create ad blocks that you can use throughout your site that other sites can pay to utilize. You can also select payments based on per ad in a variety of manners such as through CPM (cost per thousand impressions). Applying this method, you get paid a flat fee per thousand website pageviews for a specific ad. The rates can range between $1 to $3 and this rate can go higher based on niche categories. Another way which you can do this is through CPC which is cost-per-click. This way, you get paid each time an ad is clicked on your site. The rates for this vary between one industry to the other.

- AdThrive

Getting money from Adsense is slightly tough, but if you have a good website, Adsense can give you a second revenue stream no doubt. What if you're only making a few dollars in ads and only have about 1,000 website visitors? You can also use AdThrive to optimize your ads so you get better performance. AdThrive delves deep into your analytics to understand the advertisers who have the best performance on your site. From this, you can see higher CTRs on your ads and this will enable you to generate more revenue.

- InfusionSoft

InfusionSoft is a paid software and a little on the pricey end, but it is a powerful tool to use for any marketer and manager. Its finest feature is the automation that makes extremely efficient marketing campaigns for you. InfusionSoft is a robust yet costly email marketing tool that would benefit any small business looking towards reaching out to a bigger audience. The startup fee for this software is at $2,000. After this, maintenance would cost anywhere between $199 to $599 a month depending on the package you choose.

In brief, InfusionSoft saves you plenty of time. For first time users, it takes a little while to learn how to use the system and set it up according to your needs. But once setup is completed, you are pretty much set up for a smooth ride. InfusionSoft is renowned for its high deliverability rates and its ability to scale no matter what the size of the campaign.

- Keyhole

Keyhole offers a detailed analysis of the hashtags that you use for your marketing campaign. Instead of randomly using hashtags with your campaigns, Keyhole enables you to track and analyze hashtags in real time, shows you how influential it is, as well as its engagement, reach and popularity. The trial is free, but paid versions start at$132 to $799 a month. Let's face it- marketing campaigns nowadays thrive on hashtags. Not only can you track hashtags, but you can also get analytics by account, keywords, mentions and URL. This is a useful tool to have if you are always working on marketing campaigns targeting heavy social media users.

- Buzzsumo

Buzzsumo enables marketers to source the most shared content on specific topics and websites. Marketers can also refine lists according to the type of content such as blog posts, news items, or just infographics. The advanced feature includes 'monitoring' and 'influencers' that marketers can use to get ahead of the competition. The free version of Buzzsumo gives you limited results. However, the pro version starter plan is ideal for small businesses and bloggers, as it costs $99/month. But if you want something deeper and significant, then the Advanced feature at $299/month comes with API access and many more incredible features.

Content marketers would love this because it helps in searching for trending topics and subjects on the internet easier and plus, it allows content creators to analyze headlines for their effectiveness. Buzzsumo helps content marketers understand how to create the next viral topic.

- CoSchedule

CoSchedule is a software that helps you plan, organize and manage your marketing campaigns, your content and your strategies. Any marketing campaign needs to be planned and executed according to schedule, and with CoSchedule, you can streamline this process easily. CoShedule works great with Chrome, Google Docs, Wordpress and Evernote too! Coschedule ranges from $15 per month for personal use to $600 per month for larger agency users. Coshedule allows you to stay organized and it saves time. It is excellent for large companies or small agencies to manage deadlines, share notes, stay up on to their day to day tasks and get updates on campaign progress. Timelines are easier to manage, any alerts are prompted by CoSchedule.

- Pingdom Website Speed Test

Website speed is a crucial element in retaining a user's visit to your site. Website speed is one of the fastest ways to improve your SEO rankings and increase conversion rates. With Pingdom's, marketers can test their website speed, and it also gives a free report that gives you an in-depth analysis of your site as well as tips to improve it. The test itself is free however for a full on website monitoring service; it will cost you anywhere from $13.95 to $454 per month.

Full-time monitoring is essential and useful for large websites that receive plenty of traffic. A few more minutes of downtime or crash can cost you revenue as well as traffic. You can save a lot of money by investing in a monthly plan with Pingdom to continuously check your websites' status, give you alerts and monitor and report on site speed.

- Canva

With easy to use designing software available to us, most of our company's basic design materials can be made ourselves because let's face it: not everyone can afford a graphic designer on a retainer basis. If Adobe Photoshop and Illustrator is too complicated to us, then Canva is an easier alternative that makes design easy and fast. Canva has templates that are created especially for social media sharing and posting, and these templates are stunning. A few clicks here and there and you have eye-popping visual.

If you use its cloud-based software, it costs nothing. But there are premium features that come, and it is a 'pay-as-you-go 'method. If you feel your business needs constant designing but hiring a graphic designer is too much, then opt for Canva For Work. It has advanced features and a variety of other tools that you can utilize for a mere monthly subscription of $12.95.

Great visual design can create a huge impact on your target market so if you are embarking on a big marketing campaign, do not skimp on hiring a graphic designer. But if you need visual content quickly and it's something that you can easily put together quickly, then Canva will help you make your content look stunning.

Conclusion

So how do you feel now that you've covered the most relevant details of affiliate marketing? Ready to start? Well, I'm hoping that you do! Affiliate marketing takes time to build, and it depends entirely on your level of commitment- how involved you are with your marketing and promotions and how much money you want to make. If you want to make more money, then you need to invest time and effort to get things off the ground.

Starting up is a little hard simply because you need time to understand things, the mechanics of how it runs and so on. But once you have covered the bases, you are good to go! Also reading as much as you can (which includes this book) helps you build a solid foundation of affiliate marketing. Building your credibility is the most important thing in affiliate marketing, next to creating good content. With the arsenal of excellent content as well as credibility, working your way towards a consistent and increasing profit base is achievable.

Thank You

Before you go, I just wanted to say thank you for purchasing my book.

You could have picked from dozens of other books on the same topic but you took a chance and chose this one.

So, a HUGE thanks to you for getting this book and for reading all the way to the end.

Now I wanted to ask you for a small favor. **Could you please consider posting a review on the platform? Reviews are one of the easiest ways to support the work of independent authors.**

This feedback will help me continue to write the type of books that will help you get the results you want. So if you enjoyed it, please let me know!

Lastly, don't forget to grab a copy of your Free Bonuses *"The Fastest Way to Make Money with Affiliate Marketing" and "Top 10 Affiliate Offers to Promote"*. Just go to the link below.

https://theartofmastery.com/chandler-free-gift

Lightning Source UK Ltd.
Milton Keynes UK
UKHW021948220622
404832UK00003B/108